To my husband Vadim
For your unconditional love toward me.
There is no one else I would rather do life with than you.

To all those who need peace, healing, and hope
Know you are not alone.
God has a mighty plan for your life.

Contents

Free Gift

As a way of saying thanks for your purchase,
I'm offering a free gift that will help you practically
apply what you will learn in this book:

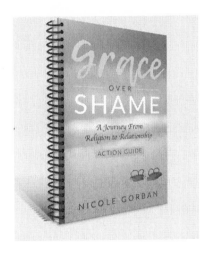

Visit the following link to access the FREE Action Guide:

https://mailchi.mp/70f364d57cf9/free-action-guide

"The Spirit of the Sovereign Lord is on me, because the Lord has anointed me to proclaim good news to the poor. He has sent me to bind up the brokenhearted, to proclaim freedom for the captives and release from darkness for the prisoners, to proclaim the year of the Lord's favor and the day of vengeance of our God, to comfort all who mourn, and provide for those who grieve in Zion—to bestow on them a crown of beauty instead of ashes, the oil of joy instead of mourning, and a garment of praise instead of a spirit of despair. They will be called oaks of righteousness, a planting of the Lord for the display of his splendor. They will rebuild the ancient ruins and restore the places long devastated; they will renew the ruined cities that have been devastated for generations. Strangers will shepherd your flocks; foreigners will work your fields and vineyards. And you will be called priests of the Lord, you will be named ministers of our God. You will feed on the wealth of nations, and in their riches you will boast. Instead of your shame you will receive a double portion, and instead of disgrace you will rejoice in your inheritance. And so you will inherit a double portion of your land and everlasting joy will be yours. For I, the Lord, love justice."

— Isaiah 61:1-8 New International Version

Foreword

Talking about *grace* is never enough. Why is it so hard for us, as people, to receive things for free? Why is it difficult to simply receive when a friend offers to pay for coffee or dinner? Why do we feel like we have to return favors, gifts, help, or support we receive from others? There are those few who take advantage of the kindness of others, but we do not like those free loaders. Most of us have a very hard time with free things. More so when it comes to unseen things of the heart.

From the beginning, the first man and woman forsake what was offered them for free and hid in shame. They still spoke with God out of the bushes though, and we too can have a relationship with God and still be in hiding by things that have happened to us, or things we have done.

In this book, Nicole exposes many lies that could take root in our hearts, sometimes through unwanted or unforeseen circumstances, often outside of our control. Nevertheless, they take root and bloom in our lives and we could mistaken them for our identity and our beliefs. Nicole's story interwoven with

God's truth is a great example of surrendering and allowing the Lord to actually be Lord so He could change and shift things in the heart that has been handed over to Him. I have known Nicole since we were toddlers, as our parents and grandparents were friends back in St. Petersburg, Russia. It has been an honor for me to witness her life and journey, her transformation and endless energy to impact women and the next generation. This book touched some depths in my own heart, and I pray that through Nicole's honesty, you will invite the Holy Spirit to search your own heart and show you if there are hidden things that He wants you to see and surrender to Him. It is the *truth* that sets us free, and it is *the truth* that we are often so afraid of.

Natasha Kosachevich

Introduction

Out of Bondage

> *"For the creation was subjected to frustration, not by its own choice, but by the will of the one who subjected it, in hope that the creation itself will be liberated from its bondage to decay and brought into the freedom and glory of the children of God."*
>
> **— Romans 8:20-21**

It was another Sunday when my husband and I quietly left the house before any of our kids woke so we could attend a church service in peace. Although we were members of a church about twenty-five minutes away, the church we attended this morning was less than a minute away; it's location alone made it attractive. Moreover, we didn't have to think twice about what to wear, but threw on our comfortable Sunday best, slid into our flip-flops, and hopped over to the church, picking up a complimentary cup of coffee on our way into the worship hall. My husband and I loved these early date-like mornings together.

This particular Sunday we heard testimonies of people going through Regeneration, which is a Biblically based twelve-step discipleship for healing, recovery, and freedom from any kind of struggle. I had never heard of this program before, but it piqued my interest, in part because I had been going through a stressful season at work and felt like my life was out of control.

Don't get me wrong; from an outside perspective, there were no signs that my life was in disorder. I had a successful career and thoroughly enjoyed my job working for a school district. I was in my fourth year supporting teachers and educational leaders to help improve the climate and culture of school campuses. Prior to that, I had been a classroom teacher for ten years, and I'd fully enjoyed impacting the lives of the kids I'd taught.

I was also a women's ministry director at my church, organizing ladies' events, women and girls' groups, as well as various retreats and trainings. I had just given up leading a women's Bible study that I had run for the last ten years. I had done that so I could focus more on leader development and the women's ministry overall.

As far as family was concerned, I was raising four beautiful daughters and my long-awaited boy, who had recently turned two. My husband and I had been happily married for fifteen years at the time, and during those years, we'd both worked hard on developing our careers. I got my teaching credential, master's degree, and administrative credential while growing our family. My husband got his bachelor's degree and was in a program to become an X-ray technologist. We had bought a house a few years back and everything seemed perfect.

But was it really?

That morning, when I heard people sharing their struggles in church and describing how Regeneration was a place for people who were going through divorce, struggling with addiction, or experiencing emotional issues, I wanted to check it out. However, a fear struck me—Going to a place where people went for recovery had to mean I needed recovery.

Was I broken?

Was I struggling?

But wasn't I a Christian?

The thoughts came fast. Christians are supposed to be the salt and light of the world. We aren't supposed to struggle with sin; we are supposed to overcome sin and not live in it any longer. Was there sin in my life that I couldn't overcome? How could I possibly admit that when I was a church leader? And if I did, would my friends and family even understand my struggle?

Though plagued by these questions, I gathered my courage and stepped into the Regeneration building the following Monday night. I did not expect to see so many people. I thought the program was only for *those* people, the ones who needed serious help. My struggle was not that serious, and all I wanted was to see what this program was about. After all, I probably could figure out how to help myself without a program, as I always had done.

As soon as I sat down, a friendly lady noticed me and took the seat next to me. She walked me through the process of what I could expect from the program, which relieved me of my anxiety. It was only her second month there, but she loved it. I felt welcome but still hesitant.

I sat through the big group session where many different people shared their testimonies. I learned later that I came on a commencement night where people who finished the program had an opportunity to share their testimonies. It was very powerful, and I was in tears because I felt right at home.

I had never heard people be so open about their struggles in church. The stories kept coming, and all of them had a very similar theme about God's grace and the healing power available for anyone no matter the struggle. These people were not finished yet as God continued working in their lives. Each story gave me overwhelming hope.

After the commencement, everyone went to their small group sessions. Since I was new, I went to the newcomers' group where they explained the program. There, they split us into two groups—ladies in one room and gentlemen in another. We sat in a circle and were asked to share why we had come.

This was uncomfortable for me because I was not expecting to share my life with strangers. I remember listening to other people talk and being amazed by how open they were. You see, I grew up in a community where sharing your feelings was discouraged, that people didn't need to know the yucky stuff we were dealing with. No one needed to know our deep wounds and sins because it could cause them to look at us differently or make them feel uncomfortable. We just needed to give our struggles and sins to God, and He would forgive us and help us get over it.

When it was time for me to speak, all I could say was, "I am here because everyone around me seems to be okay, but I'm not okay. I'm here to figure out what is wrong with me and allow God to work in me through this process."

Have you ever felt like me, afraid to let anyone know what is *really* going on inside you? Afraid people will judge you or think less of you? You live trapped by your past, defeated by your struggles, pretending to be okay. You can't be completely honest with anyone because you think they will never understand you. You keep telling yourself to get over it, to get a grip, try harder, be better. You tell yourself you are completely in control. You make grand promises to yourself and somehow always find excuses to not follow through on them. You feel as though you are on a treadmill, running faster and faster yet staying in the same place. You are tired and you want to be free from the constant effort of trying to perform, trying to be happy and trying to make everyone else happy, all while you feel that your efforts are never enough.

If that's you, if that's your reality, this book is for you.

I will share my journey from running on this religious treadmill for many years, desperately trying to overcome my struggles on my own while at the same time pretending those struggles did not exist. Until, finally, I got off the treadmill to find freedom in a relationship with Jesus Christ. It took me most of my life to understand who God is and who I am in Him. When I finally did, I found the purpose, peace, and power to live by faith. My life has been transformed by the truths I will explain in this book, which, if you believe in them, will also transform your life.

If you are someone who grew up in a strict, legalistic church, this book will help you comprehend why you feel powerless in overcoming your struggles. It will also answer some questions and doubts you may have had, or maybe still have, about things you learned growing up. Additionally, it will assist you in gaining freedom from a legalistic mentality so you can live by faith that is rooted in a deep and meaningful relationship with Jesus.

If you are someone who did not grow up in church, was pushed away, or just walked away for whatever reason, this book will help you understand what Christianity is all about, who God really is, and who you really are when you put your faith in Christ. It will answer some of your questions about faith and lead you to the truth that will set you free from the effects of sin and shame.

If you are someone who grew up in a non-legalistic church, especially if you are a church leader, this book will help you acknowledge the misconceptions people have to help them find freedom, healing, peace, and purpose. It will reaffirm your faith and deepen your relationship with the Lord.

I hope as you read the coming chapters, you will understand that you are not alone in your struggles. I pray that God would open your heart to hear what He wants to say to you through my story and the truths I learned about Him. It is not my intent to cause a theological debate or to offend anyone but to share my personal experience of coming to Christ. I ask that you read this book with the eyes of grace because it is not easy to share my deepest secrets and struggles, but I hope that through this, I can testify about God's amazing grace, which reaches the darkest corners of the human heart. Most importantly, I hope that through my story, you can comprehend the danger of legalism and work-based salvation. I feel deeply that even if this book helps one person find freedom in Christ, the effort was well worth it.

Chapter 1

I Am Not Okay

> *"For I know that nothing good lives in me, that is, in my sinful nature. For I have the desire to do what is good, but I cannot carry it out."*
>
> **— Romans 7:18**

You might be wondering about the struggle that propelled me to join a recovery program. Honestly, I'm hesitant to share it now, just as I was to share it with my group in the Regeneration program that first Monday night. Even today, I have not met many people who share the same challenge. It is a struggle that, unless they have also lived it, not many people understand. And even those who have experienced it often do not want to talk about it due to shame. So instead, they keep it private and hidden, trying to work on it in their own strength. Dr. Brené Brown, a research professor at the University of Houston's Graduate College of Social Work, who has spent a big portion of her life studying the topic, defines shame as "the intensely painful feeling or experience of believing we are flawed and therefore unworthy of acceptance and belonging."[1]

But this was my truth: I was struggling with an eating disorder, which made me feel like something was terribly wrong with me. I felt like I was broken and flawed.

I am not sure exactly how it started, but I have one vivid memory of an incident in my life that was possibly a building block to this struggle. I was around the age of six and my parents were headed to a New Year's party, which happened to be at my best friend's house, where they would be all night with my two older siblings. It was a custom for us to stay up all night celebrating the new year with activities and games, and the kids always had a blast while the parents socialized. That year, I desperately wanted to go, and I cried bitterly, begging my parents to take me.

Since my parents were determined to only take two kids and leave me and my younger siblings at home with Grandma, my mom gave me a chocolate bar as a consolation gift. I remember how I stopped crying and ate it in its entirety that very night. I couldn't remember when I had a whole chocolate bar to myself; we kids often had to share because there were seven of us. So that night, chocolate was my comfort that took away the sadness I felt at being left at home.

The more I think about it, it wasn't just chocolate that brought me comfort in times of need back then, but food in general. Not all food, of course, just the good and yummy foods like pasta, breads, and sweets. Pea soup, for example, never brought me comfort, or joy for that matter, but homemade pirogue always did. My mom was a great cook—still is—and the smell of her cooking brought a sense of warmth, peace, and comfort to our home, especially when she baked.

The whole house would fill with an aroma that made you run to the kitchen. I especially loved when she baked *plushki,* which are a Russian version of little cinnamon rolls, except they are rolled on both sides and look like owl eyes when cut and laid out. Resisting those was impossible because they smelled like sweet cinnamon and were doughy, soft yet crisp, sugary, and had shiny edges that pulled you into taking a bite. One bite and all your resistance crumbled. And she didn't just bake these heavenly goodies. She baked poppyseed rolls, sweet cream cheese pastries, sweet crepes, and heavenly cakes. If there was an award to give for the best cook, I would give it to my mom.

My mom's cooking always brought the family together in the kitchen where we shared laughter, stories, and our latest jokes. The kitchen was an escape haven where all our worries melted away and the joy of family and togetherness was truly felt. It was free of fighting, free of punishment, free of pain. We felt safe in the kitchen. We felt loved in the kitchen. We felt accepted and cared for in the kitchen. Sure, there were conflict and painful disagreements happening in our house from time to time, but they happened in other places in the house, not the kitchen, at least in my recollection.

As I got older, the kitchen continued being my escape and food my comfort when dealing with strong emotions. Somehow, eating a gooey doughnut took away my anxiety—at least for a moment. Somehow, filling up on chicken pasta alfredo filled my emptiness—at least for a moment. Somehow, slowly slurping a vanilla ice-cream shake shaved my fear away and gave me a sense of peace—at least for a moment. At least for a moment, I could escape back into my mom's kitchen filled with love, peace, and comfort.

One thing about getting older you never think about until it hits you is puberty. Well, maybe you do think about it, but you have no idea what is about to happen, especially if no one ever warned you. At the time, I learned some things from friends, some from Mom, and others I just figured out—and one of those things I just figured out was weight gain. I honestly never considered that weight gain would affect me since all of my life I had been extremely skinny and athletic. I hardly ever ate and often experienced stomach issues because I would forget to eat. However, as my mom can testify, when it came to eating foods I loved, I could eat three portions at a time.

It was a surprise to me that when I started my sophomore year in high school, my weight started to climb. I began watching what I was eating, but I still loved my comfort food because it helped me get through the day and overcome the stress of school. I remember one day I was talking to a friend in the bathroom about how I should not have eaten a brownie we baked in cooking class since I was trying to lose weight. She told me I could throw up the food I didn't want and stop obsessing about it.

I had never thought about throwing up food before. At first, the whole idea disgusted me, bringing back memories of when I had the stomach flu, but still, I thought I'd give it a try, especially since my friend had done it, and she seemed fine— and happy with her weight. I told myself my guilt of eating the brownie would be gone along with the unwanted calories, and it would just be this once.

Little did I know that this single incident would put me in an eating disorder prison for the next seven years. I thought I was in control. I thought I could enjoy the foods that brought me comfort and then flush the calories down the toilet. But what I quickly realized was, though it offered me the feeling of control, I was actually completely out of control.

Yes, there were better days, days when I felt great and did not turn to food for comfort. Days when life was beautiful. But there were many days, which I will talk about later in this book, when life was bitter, and food was my escape—at least for a moment.

Seven years after the brownie incident, I got married to a wonderful guy who had no idea about my struggle. While we dated, I hid this sickness well and could go days without an episode, especially if I ate clean. I exercised, dieted, and did whatever I could to control my eating, but it would still sneak in at the most unexpected time. But not after our wedding. I am not sure exactly how I recovered, but I'd venture to say my husband had something to do with it. Not one incident in fifteen years. Not one.

Fast forward to August 2018. I had been given a new project at work with high levels of stress, and I started experiencing fear and anxiety about my work. I felt overwhelmed by the complexity of some tasks and the expected outcomes and was putting a lot of pressure on myself to perform, and perform well, though much was out of my control.

In the midst of anxiety, I have turned to ice-cream for comfort. It wasn't anything new. In fact, I often treated myself with sweets, but I had gotten good about keeping it to a minimum because I had just lost all the baby weight after having my son and was in the best shape of my life. But this time, as I spooned the ice cream into my mouth, the out-of-control feeling took over and I was compulsively eating, unable to stop. I ate till I was extremely uncomfortable. And then I relapsed, which terrified me. All the memories from my past engulfed me. I did not want to go back to that prison of binging and purging.

This was why I started the recovery program. I did not relapse entirely but the mentality began to again control me and the fear of a complete relapse, the fear of weight gain, and the fear of failure at work pushed me over the edge. I felt like I was losing control and if I didn't do something about it, things could go from bad to worse. I was afraid of my own ability to cause havoc on my life. I didn't want to be fearful and anxious. I prayed and asked God to take away my fear and anxiety. While I meditated on His words, I felt peace, but the negative feelings didn't leave. I was still anxious and fearful, and now with an added out-of-control feeling, I felt hopeless and depressed. I was not okay.

But who could I tell? Who would understand? In the past, if I had told anyone about my feelings, I would get these responses:

- You need to get over it! You have nothing to be anxious about!

- You need to control it!

- You need to trust God more!

- You need to pray and read the Bible more!

- *Возьми себя в руки!* That's in Russian, in case you didn't understand, meaning *get a grip*.

And though all of those things sounded like the right things to do, they were not working. I couldn't get over it, nor could I control it. I tried giving it to God, but it seemed like He gave it right back. I was still anxious, still fearful, and still struggling to not go back to my eating disorder prison.

Have you ever felt like your body was not listening to you? You wanted to do the right thing but did the opposite instead. You wanted to be kind but ended up saying something you regretted. You wanted to get up early, but just couldn't get yourself up. You wanted to eat healthy but ended up eating junk. You wanted to be calm but ended up screaming at your kids, because that's the only way to get them to listen. You wanted to organize your house, but the energy or motivation was lacking. You wanted to quit a bad habit but ended up doing it even more.

This reminds me of a passage in the Bible where Apostle Paul shared a similar struggle. He wrote about it in Romans 7:18, "I know that nothing good lives in me, that is, in my sinful nature. For I have the desire to do what is good, but I cannot carry it out." This was someone who wrote over half of the New Testament. He was called an apostle, someone who was commissioned as an authority figure to teach and preach. He was supposed to have it all together. He was supposed to be in control. He was supposed to get over his struggles and be a role model for other Christ followers. Yet, he admitted his struggles, his temptations to do what was evil, and his inability to do what was good.

As I sat in a circle at Regeneration with about twenty ladies that first Monday night as they admitted their struggles, I could not help but wonder what it would be like if this was possible at my church with the people I so dearly loved. I wondered how different church would be if people really knew each other, not just the outside façade, but really knew each other. And not only knew, but loved one another with all of their flaws, all of their failures, all of their insecurities, and all of their secret struggles and sins—just as Jesus loves us.

Would that even be possible?

It is easy to love people you know very little about, who have it all together, or only struggle with the *acceptable* sins that many of us struggle with, like outbursts of anger or anxiety. Those issues are just part of our human experience. We can all admit to struggling with one of these issues at one point or another in our lives, or maybe even struggling with these consistently, but we often don't condemn people for them because we would all be guilty, whether we admit it or not.

But could you love someone if you knew their secret sins? Could you love someone who struggles with drug addiction? Could you love someone who struggles with sexual immorality? Could you love someone who struggles with thoughts about hurting their kids? Could you love someone who struggles with alcoholism? What about someone who struggles with an eating disorder and either starves themselves, binges, or purges food? Could you love someone who struggles with same-sex attraction? What about someone who struggles with self-harm? Suicidal thoughts?

The list goes on. Maybe I did not mention your struggle or maybe you are not aware of your struggle. What I am trying to convey here is that we live in a broken world filled with broken people who have habits they are trying to break, hang-ups they are trying to overcome, and hurts they are trying to forget and

19

move on from. We all struggle with something that may or may not be obvious to others and sometimes it isn't even obvious to us.

The question is: How do we break free? How do we overcome these habits, hang-ups, and hurts? How do we live a life of freedom and purpose? I'd love to answer this question right here and now with one word.

JESUS

But it isn't that simple to understand, especially if you are not a Jesus follower. And even if you do call yourself a Christian, this is still something many people grapple with. How is Jesus the answer to everything? This is what I wrestled with all of my life as I grew up going to church. Truthfully, I'm only now beginning to understand what this really means. Only He can transform our lives, give us freedom, and fill our need for love. I will help you understand more truths in the next chapters, but I do want to start with the most important truth that helped me cast out the lie I was believing that I could somehow fix myself. We can never fix ourselves, even if we try really hard. Jesus is the only solution for our brokenness.

Jesus did not come to earth to show us *how* to fix or save ourselves, as many religions of this world do by outlining their requirements for access and status maintenance. Instead, Jesus fulfilled all of the requirements by living a perfect life. Then He died on our behalf, taking the punishment we fully deserve for our sins, and becoming the way of salvation for us, giving us an eternal status of being God's children. He Himself became our way to eternity and freedom from our brokenness.

It is not religious duties and disciplines that save you, it is the person Jesus. The gospel of John 14:6 records Jesus as saying, "I'm the way and the truth and the life. No one comes to the Father except through me." He made a way for us to have peace with God through a relationship with Him. Why is this important? Because you can miss Jesus and miss eternity if you don't grasp this. Salvation and solution for our brokenness are delivered through a relationship with Jesus, not through good behavior and fulfillment of religious requirements.

Timothy Keller in his book *The Reason for God & The Prodigal God* explains this well. He describes what I have discovered through personal experience, which is why it resonated with me. He states, "Sin and evil are self-centeredness and pride that lead to oppression against others, but there are two forms of this. One form is being very bad and breaking all the rules, and the other form is being very good and keeping all the rules and becoming self-righteous."[2] It makes sense to most of us that if you take the path of breaking all the rules and deny Jesus, you will not be saved, and your life will continue to revolve in brokenness. But it is harder to understand why following all the rules would be a path to a possibility of not being saved and not having a solution for brokenness.

If you are not a Christian but have always tried to live a moral lifestyle—meaning you haven't killed anyone, have been faithful in your relationships, and have even contributed to the good of others—it seems like there should be some reward in that. Yet, without a relationship with Jesus, all these things are worthless when it comes to eternity. They might give you a sense of satisfaction and purpose in life, but they will not give you eternal life. You will still have to pay a penalty for your sins because no one is perfect without Jesus. And that penalty is eternal punishment apart from God.

Jesus set the bar really high for what it means to be good in God's eyes. God is holy and requires absolute perfection. However, we as humans will always fall short even in our most extreme efforts. For example, you may not have murdered anyone, but have you ever gotten angry with someone? You may never have committed adultery, but have you ever had a sexual thought? You may never have said a foul word, but have you ever thought foul thoughts? The Bible says, in Matthew 5:21, "You have heard that it was said to the people long ago, 'You shall not murder, and anyone who murders will be subject to judgment.' But I tell you that anyone who is angry with a brother or sister will be subject to judgment." How many of you can honestly say you have never gotten angry with anyone? I know I can't! I already missed the bar of perfection.

If you are a Christian, you might agree you have done these things and you have missed the mark; this is why you accepted Jesus's sacrifice. However, you may be focusing on trying to maintain your status by following certain rules that have nothing to do with faith, which means the relationship you have with Jesus is solely based on your ability to perform. Your idea of a good Christian is based on good behavior and Biblical knowledge. You compare yourself to others, thinking you are more spiritual because you behave better. You judge others for their inability to live morally. You are shocked when people commit certain sins while being Christians. And the worst part of it is, you condemn people for falling into one of the unacceptable sins like adultery, drugs, or alcoholism. In John 3:17, it says, "For God did not send his Son into the world to condemn the world, but to save the world through him." This is where you can also miss Jesus: by living a moral lifestyle, keeping all the rules, and doing all the right things, but still playing God, judging and condemning others, when even God did not send His Son to condemn, but to save. In a sense, you have become self-righteous and arrogant by keeping all the rules. You have become your own Lord and Savior.[3]

This is not to say that living a moral lifestyle and following the commands of God isn't important. It just means that living your life in a moral way in order to somehow acquire or maintain a standing with God is being your own Savior. No matter how upstanding your actions, there is nothing you can do to save yourself or fix yourself and nothing you can do to maintain your position. It is freely given to you by faith. If we see this gift as transactional—meaning we have to do something to maintain being worthy of the gift—we can become like the Pharisees, who put their trust in the law instead of Jesus.

Jesus speaks boldly to them in Matthew 12:34, "You brood of vipers, how can you who are evil say anything good? For the mouth speaks what the heart is full of." You see, on the outside, the Pharisees looked extremely righteous, wearing appropriate clothing, observing certain rituals, following the law to the letter. But on the inside, they were filled with hypocrisy, trying to appear righteous, yet always feeling insecure because trying to live a perfect life takes effort, and involves never feeling like enough. In fact, the Pharisees weren't enough and could never be enough without Jesus.

Apostle Paul, known as Saul before his conversion, was also a Pharisee who searched out Christians and murdered them because of their faith in Jesus. When Jesus met him on the way to Damascus, as described in Acts 9:4-5, he asked, "'Saul, Saul, why do you persecute me?' 'Who are you, Lord?' Saul asked." This is a person who thought he was doing God's work, who thought he has kept all the rules, yet he had no idea who Jesus was. He was so busy following all the rules that he literally missed Jesus.

There is also a story in Matthew 25:1-12 about ten virgins who were waiting for their bridegroom, half of whom were wise and half of whom were foolish. The foolish ones didn't take extra oil with them to keep their lamps running, and since the bridegroom took longer than expected, they were running out. They asked the wise virgins to give them some oil, but the wise virgins told them to go buy their own so they would all have enough. While these foolish virgins were gone, the bridegroom came, and the wise virgins went into the wedding banquet. Later when the foolish virgins came, they said, "Open the door for us," but he replied, "I tell you the truth, I don't know you."

You see, it is not about rule following or, like the story of the virgins, having the lamp, because they all had the lamps. From an outside perspective, they were all waiting for the bridegroom. Externally, they looked and behaved as if they were all going to the banquet, but it wasn't enough. That was the difference. The wise women had enough oil, while the foolish didn't. There are many interpretations of this story, which I am not going to get into, but in the end, we see that the wise women *were known* by the bridegroom, while the foolish *weren't*. The only thing you need in order to be enough to enter into eternity with God is a relationship with a God who *knows* you. This relationship comes from *faith* in Jesus Christ and *acceptance* of His death for your brokenness and sin.

Matthew 7:22-23 talks about this same idea. "Many will say to me on that day, 'Lord, Lord, did we not prophesy in your name and in your name drive out demons and, in your name, perform many miracles?' Then I will tell them plainly, 'I never knew you. Away from me, you evildoers!'" I find this especially disturbing because I would never want to be in this position, thinking I was doing all these things in God's name, when in fact, God never knew me. These people were called evildoers even though they were doing all these amazing acts. Why? Because they did not accept Jesus and instead relied on their own strength. They did not have a relationship with God.

There are many religions today that focus on self-effort salvation, and sometimes even Christianity can inadvertently encourage it. Many people cling to religion because it has a way of helping them be better people, clean up their lives, or do the right things, but as I said earlier, it is still their own work, own effort, in trying to reach a certain level of righteousness that would make them good enough to deserve eternal life. No one can be saved without Jesus. Thus, quit believing the lie that you can somehow help yourself. Instead, embrace the truth that the solution is only found in Jesus.

Lie #1:	I can fix my brokenness if I try really hard.
Truth #1:	Jesus is the only solution for my brokenness.

Before you turn the page to the next chapter, reflect on the following questions:

1. How have you tried to fix your own issues? What was the outcome?

2. Do you worry about what other people would think if they truly knew you?

3. What evidence in your life suggests that you have a relationship with Jesus?

4. If you don't have a relationship with Jesus, what stops you from accepting His gift?

Chapter 2

Growing up Confused

> *"Everyone who has been born of God does not sin, because His seed remains in him; he is not able to sin, because he has been born of God. This is how God's children and the devil's children become obvious."*
>
> **— 1 John 3:9-10 (Christian Standard Bible)**

I was born on October 29, 1980, in St. Petersburg, Russia, during a time of religious persecution. God was proclaimed non-existent and atheism was established as the religion of the state and the supreme truth. Anyone who criticized atheism was subject to severe punishment in the form of torture, concentration camps, mental institutions, and even death.[4] Since the birth of the Soviet Union in 1917, persecutions had varied in intensity, and the year I was born they were escalating, as I learned from my parents. The KGB, the Russian intelligence and internal-security service, was actively working to catch churchgoers in the midst of service and arrest leaders. They had spies within the church who pretended they were Christians, learned about all the secret meetings, and then reported everything to the authorities. Christian homes were searched, all Bibles and Christian literature confiscated if found, and threats imposed. Our church was undergoing persecution to the point where we had to hide in the forest for gatherings. Even then, police would find us and arrest our leaders.

When I was eight months old, my grandfather on my mom's side, who was a pastor of our church, was taken to a labor camp in Siberia to serve a five-year sentence. When he was released, I remember going to the airport to meet him; he picked me up in his arms and couldn't believe how much I had grown. His love for God and genuine love for people around him was evident. I will never forget his many visits to our house as he brought bread and milk along with other goodies, always with an encouraging word and a contagious smile. For some reason, even though I was a child, I always felt like he saw more in me; he never focused on my behavior, though I wasn't the most behaved of children, but rather saw me as a child of God. He and my grandma fasted and prayed for us every Wednesday, from what my mom told me, and I probably would not be where I am today if it wasn't for their prayers.

After his five-year sentence, my grandfather went right back to preaching even though the authorities threatened him that he could be sent away for good. This didn't stop him, and he continued to spread the good news. My grandfather has demonstrated great faith in times of persecution and left a legacy for our family about the importance of preaching the gospel no matter the circumstances. Christian Cinema created a movie titled *Captive Faith*, which describes my grandfather's experience along with two other pastors who were sentenced in Siberia, where despite severe treatment, they never stopped proclaiming the gospel.[5]

Living in the midst of persecutions was frightening. I have numerous memories of police interrupting our services and dragging people away. One particular Christmas, as we gathered for a children's service not very far from the city, soldiers surrounded the house with rifles. They knocked on the door and said they would start shooting if we didn't let them in. The doors were opened, and they marched us down to the station. As we walked in the middle of a cold winter evening with snow shimmering on both sides and metal rifles clicking nearby, the adults secretly decided to grab their kids and run in different directions. On the count of three, everyone scattered, and my two siblings and I ran with my dad to the nearest train station and safely made it home. What an experience! They did catch a few people, who were arrested, and some even imprisoned.

Both my parents grew up in Christian families and were used to being mocked for their faith in school and then, as they got older, at work and other places if people knew they were Christian. My mom still remembers standing up to a teacher when she was trying to prove that there was no God. The teacher claimed, "Since Eve was made out of Adam's rib, every man should have a missing rib. Since men nowadays do not have missing ribs, there must be no God." My mom confronted the teacher, saying, "So do you think that someone who is born without a leg or who had their leg cut off would have kids without legs?" That definitely made the teacher pause, but she called my mom some insulting word and moved on with the lesson.

Christians were not able to get a higher education unless they joined the communist party. They could only get a technical education and even then, they would face difficulties getting a job that would support their family. My dad was a television mechanic and my mom a nurse, but I hardly remember her working, while my dad was often away on work trips. In addition to that, they cleaned territories around the city, from snow in the winter to leaves in the fall, which was a common practice in Russia for keeping the city clean, and it helped pay for our food. Life was not easy for my parents, but even in these challenging circumstances, they never complained, but did everything they could to make us happy.

While it seems contrary, but even in the midst of trials and persecutions, the church took an active part in spreading the good news about Jesus. Even children in Sunday school went out onto the streets to preach the gospel. I was one of those kids and became quite an evangelist. Our Sunday school class did not meet during church but at someone's house after church, and it was something I always looked forward to. As we traveled from train to bus to trolleybus, we talked to people about Jesus and passed out little salvation booklets. We told people about how much God loved them and wanted them to be saved from sin and hell, and we had a lot of fun doing it because we were with our friends. The verse in John 3:16, "For God so loved the world that he gave his one and only Son, that whoever believes in him shall not perish but have eternal life" became a verse I knew by heart.

I was also evangelizing to my friends at school whenever I got a chance, though I did not fully understand what it meant to be saved. I just knew that Jesus came and died for us so that we would not have to go to hell. When my friends asked me about what it meant to be saved, or what it meant to be a Christian, I told them what I understood at that time. I said that when you become a Christian, you don't paint your nails, you don't put makeup on, you cannot wear pants or cut your hair if you're a woman; if you're a man, you don't grow your hair. You don't watch TV, you don't wear jewelry, even wedding rings; you don't go to theaters, dance, drink, or cuss. It was a long list of don'ts, which were considered to be sinful because they resembled the practices of the world. We were called to look different, which is why our church had that understanding. However, I do not remember my grandfather focusing on those things as much as others in the church, who made sure to call people out if someone didn't comply with certain rules. I'm not sure exactly where these influences came from, but I suspect culture played a role. But at that time, all I could do was wonder.

That being said, I was quite perplexed about some of the rules, especially when some of the things we couldn't do were written about in the Bible, like drinking wine,[6] wearing jewelry,[7] clapping,[8] and even dancing.[9] I remember attending another church—this church was considered a free church—and seeing people clap in excitement, which made me think they were doing something wrong because clapping was not allowed in our church. We had good reasons for that. You see, clapping for people was considered giving glory and praise to a person rather than God since it was people that sang in choir or preached on stage. *Why couldn't we clap for the Lord?* I reasoned. But I was too young to ask questions, so I stayed confused.

As a family, we often got together for Bible reading and prayer. I am grateful that my parents taught us how to pray and took the time to teach us about God. My parents made it a priority to read and pray with us on a daily basis. Sure, we missed a few times here and there, but for the most part it was ingrained in us that we should pray in the morning, at night, and at mealtimes. As a child, I loved the stories Mom read to us about different Bible heroes as we looked at pictures in the children's Bible. Dad often turned on audio stories, which we also enjoyed while falling asleep. When we prayed before bed, though the process of prayer was a little long because we had a large family, I saw it as important because I was afraid that if I didn't pray and say the words, "forgive me for all my sins," I would go to hell. And since I didn't know when Jesus would come, I had to make sure I said my last prayer in case He were to come that night.

As I got older, sometimes our family meetings turned into lectures about our behavior, which was probably the right thing to do as my parents wanted the best for us; however, I secretly dreaded coming to those meetings and tried to find an excuse to avoid them, especially if my behavior wasn't up to par. I developed this mentality that if I was good, my parents were pleased and loved me, but if I was bad, punishment or a lecture was just around the corner, which was all well-deserving. But so often, I was afraid to admit my wrongdoing because I was afraid of the consequences that would follow. This translated to my understanding about God, that His love and favor depended on my behavior.

When it came to church services, just like most children, I had a hard time sitting through a service. Sometimes they went past two or even three hours and kids were expected to sit in church the entire time because Sunday school was not during the service, but after. I believe this was done so children could worship together with their parents. After all, these were the times of persecution and the authorities did not want kids in church, since the plan was to brainwash the next generation into atheism. We were lucky to have been allowed to attend, thanks to my grandfather who would rather be imprisoned than to stop bringing kids to church. As a child, however, it was hard to sit through a service. Though I loved seeing my friends and going places after church, I did not understand much of what was preached. I enjoyed the singing and looked forward to times when I had to come out and recite a poem or play violin but sitting through three long sermons was challenging on a backless wooden bench, though at that time, we were lucky to even have those available. I often made excuses to go to the restroom and then found a baby to look after for a mom who wanted to sit in church. Other times, I had a stomachache and asked my mom to give me a sandwich she made for after church so she would let me leave the service and go outside to eat. I kept thinking to myself that if heaven was going to be anything like the church service, I never wanted to go there.

However, I did not want to go to hell, so I attempted to understand the messages preached in church. I knew the basic concept of God sending His Son to die on the cross for our sins, but I didn't know what it meant practically. I struggled with understanding what was supposed to happen when we believed in Jesus. There was one verse that often stood out to me and caused the most confusion. It was from 1 John 3:9-10, "Everyone who has been born of God does not sin, because His seed remains in him; he is not able to sin, because he has been born of God. This is how God's children and the Devil's children become obvious." I thought that if I believed in Jesus and repented in front of the church for my sins, then I would stop sinning completely. However, I was confused when that did not happen. I believed in Jesus pretty much since birth. How could I not believe if I grew up in a Christian family? I repented in front of the church asking Jesus to forgive all my sins and thought I was born of God. Yet I still sinned.

Am I a child of the devil?

This confusion lasted for a long time as I kept doubting my salvation. I repented again and again at church, never feeling good enough. I was afraid I would go to hell because I struggled with trying to be good but was always failing. Even if I had a really good day, I would still pray before bed asking forgiveness for everything I had possibly done wrong. Sunday after Sunday, I sat in church thinking I needed to repent again as the altar call came, but I was embarrassed to do so because I'd already done it a few times and it was supposed to be a onetime experience.

Why is it not working for me?

When I was born, my mom told me I had a really small head without a soft spot and the doctors told her that I was going to be mentally disabled since the brain had no space to grow. Well, either the doctors were wrong, or my mom's prayers were answered because I developed normally. At least that's what I thought—maybe the confusion had something to do with this? Ha-ha! Actually, I learned how to read when I was three, earlier than anyone else in my family; I started violin lessons at the age of six and when I entered first grade, I already knew some of the multiplication tables and was the fastest reader in class.

I thrived at being the best in school, in church, and even at home. I accepted nothing less of myself than straight As, always having my homework done and my materials organized. In church, I made sure I looked good in my ironed dress with my hair braided. I recited poems and loved the compliments after. I read my Bible and memorized verses they assigned in Sunday school.

I always had to be the best. If I wasn't, I would get upset with myself and try harder the next time. I wanted to be loved and accepted, and if being good and smart was going to get me that, I was ready to sacrifice everything. I developed this mentality that I had to be perfect in order for people to love and accept me. And if I could not be perfect, I got really upset. I remember how I crumpled up a whole composition book because I made a mistake writing in pen. I picked up a new notebook and did the same thing again. I was angry that I couldn't make one sheet perfect. I think I wasted at least twenty books before I was satisfied with my writing.

I also wanted my room to be perfect and when one thing was out of place, I got angry and made a bigger mess because I figured it was already messy. This all-or-nothing mentality went hand in hand with perfectionism. I got the nickname *Zamarashka*, which translates to *Cinderella*—not in the endearing way, but in the literal translation to *ash girl*, or messy. I hated that nickname because I felt like it did not define me. I wanted to be perfect, I wanted to be liked and be what people wanted me to be, yet I couldn't always make that happen, which caused thoughts of inadequacy and worthlessness.

When I played with my siblings, I always had to go first and had often already made up my mind about how this game was going to go. If something did not go my way and appeared to disrupt my perfectionistic idea, I threw away the whole day and pouted or cried in the corner. Some days I cried for hours as my family ignored me, hoping I would stop. This all-or-nothing mentality was difficult to break.

I had created a life plan in my mind—I wanted my life to be perfect—and it was supposed to play out exactly how I imagined. I hoped God would not come too soon because I wanted to get married, have children, and be a teacher. Everything had to be absolutely perfect. Period.

This perfectionistic mentality was not only toward my everyday life but toward all things related to God. This was even more important because if I wasn't perfect and died, I thought I would go straight to hell. I knew only Jesus could make me perfect, but I had to ask Him, and if I didn't get the chance or somehow failed big? Oh, I didn't want to think about that. So I tried to do everything I knew to make sure I was in good standing with God, but it never felt like enough.

Since I repented in church and didn't stop sinning, I thought maybe I would stop sinning if I read more of the Bible and prayed more often. I would read myself to exhaustion, and if I missed a day, I had to start from the beginning again because I'd ruined my perfect pattern. I often got stuck in the middle reading through all the prophets, so I skipped and went to New

Testament. Despite my endeavors, I was never able to read through the entire Bible.

Bible reading was not easy; it felt like a chore, and it did not produce the effect I was expecting in my life, which was what the verse in 1 John 3:6 had stated, "No one who lives in him keeps on sinning. No one who continues to sin has either seen him or known him." I was reading the Bible, and supposedly living in the Bible daily, but I was still sinning.

I actually struggled with one particular sin that produced the most shame in my life. I don't know my first encounter with it, but I remember being very young, maybe around three or four, and my parents rebuking me, saying not to touch down there. I didn't understand what was happening to my body, and why I wasn't supposed to touch where it felt good. I knew it was wrong, so I did it in secret. It helped me fall asleep and cope with the *monsters* that haunted me at night, whether through my dreams, or while lying wide awake in the middle of the night. I would be afraid to move because I felt as if an evil spirit was in my room.

Other nights, I would dream about demonic figures who were pulling me into the darkness as I cried "Maaaa-maaaa!" with absolutely no voice coming out of my mouth. I would see my mom and dad through a small opening in the door, as they watched TV and casually talked; however, they could not hear me screaming and being dragged away into what seemed like an abyss. These types of dreams were my reality growing up and as strange as it may sound, eventually I learned how to escape the agony of my dreams by pulling apart my eyes and wake myself up. However, being awake was still frightening in the middle of the night, so I would sooth myself back to sleep by what I now know as masturbation. At least for a moment, I'd feel relief from the terrors, but then I'd feel really guilty.

As I got older, more sins crept into my life, like stealing candy from my parents, then later, stealing money; fighting with my siblings; watching television when parents weren't home, and hiding the fact that we did when they came back.

You might think these are just normal things children go through. And yes, you are absolutely right, these might be very normal human behaviors. However, what this reveals is that we are born sinners and from very early on, we are programmed to sin. When we come to a point when we realize that we are powerless over our sins—whether it's a childish sin like fighting with siblings or stealing candy from parents, or a more mature sin like adultery or addiction—we are ready to receive what Jesus had done on the cross for us.

He defeated sin and unlocked the door to our prison. When we accept this gift and enter into a relationship with Him (even if we are still struggling with sin, because we will, as long as we are in this body), we have eternal life. Being a Christian does not mean you will not struggle with sin; it means you admit you have sin and you put your faith in Jesus, who paid for your sins and purified you from all unrighteousness, making you perfect, as if you were without sin, even in the midst of your struggles. You do not have to clean up your life before you come to

Christ. He does the work when you accept the gift of grace and allow the Holy Spirit to change your desires from the inside out. This truth was essential to my growth as a Christian. If you find yourself struggling with sin while being a Christian—whether it is a bad habit, an addiction, a sexual sin, or whatever else—know that it does not mean you are not saved.

When you start doubting your salvation, you give the enemy a foothold to do its damaging work. I doubted my salvation because I didn't fully understand what Jesus had done, and it only brought more destruction. But this is exactly what the enemy is trying to do to you—steal, kill, and destroy, as we read in John 10:10, "The thief comes only to steal and kill and destroy; I have come that they may have life, and have it to the full." The thief is the devil who wants to steal the joy of your salvation by telling you that you are good for nothing because you can't quit a certain habit or sin. He wants to kill any hope of the future because you are stuck in your past. And he wants to destroy your life so you will not walk in the purpose God has for you. He wants you to doubt your salvation because that is exactly what will keep you stuck in your sin.

But Jesus came to give you abundant life. If the devil wants to bring death to your life by keeping you stuck in your struggles with sin, Jesus wants to do the opposite. He does that by offering you Himself so that you can love Him, be protected by Him, learn from Him, and find comfort, strength, and pleasure in Him, rather than your sins. He is offering you a relationship. And when you seek to be one with Him, He will show you how to break those habits. And if you mess up, He will give you the grace and ability to get back up.

What I was missing about the verse in 1 John 3:6, was the verses that came right before, 1 John 3:4-5, "Everyone who sins breaks the law; in fact, sin is lawlessness. But you know that he appeared so that he might take away our sins. And in him is no sin." Pay close attention to the phrase *in him is no sin.* When we put our faith *in him,* we do not sin. Yes, we still struggle with sin in reality, but from God's perspective, we are sinless. It is not counted against us. Wow! That's profound news! The only way our sins count against us is if we do not believe *in him.* It is all by faith, which is what will free you from that very same sin you struggle with, this profound understanding, this faith. It may not happen right away but as you let God work in your heart and mind, He will help you.

As you walk with Jesus, your faith will grow, but you will still fall into temptation and sin. The Bible records a number of examples of people who failed in their walk or who doubted God. The most prominent Bible hero is David, I'm sure you have heard of him. He was a shepherd who was insignificant but later became a king. He was called a man after God's own heart. He wrote most of Psalms in the Bible, and if you read Psalms, you will easily see why David was called that.

He loved God with all his heart. He had an intimate relationship with God. It was not dependent on his behavior, because let me tell you, he failed big. As a king, he didn't go off to war when he was supposed to. Then, while walking around his house, he saw a beautiful woman bathing and decided to sleep with her; this woman was married, and her husband was fighting a fierce battle—the battle David was supposed to lead as king. The woman got pregnant and to cover up his mistake, David decided to call her husband back from the battle to go home to sleep with his wife to cover up the pregnancy. That didn't work out since the husband would not allow himself to relax at home while the other soldiers faced great danger. David then decided to take matters into his own hands and orchestrated the murder of the woman's husband in battle, thinking he could get away with it. It turned out he could not get away from God, and when a prophet called him on this, David immediately repented of his wrongdoing.[10] However, David still wasn't a perfect man; the Bible later describes his struggles with control,[11] deception,[12] and bitterness.[13] Yet, he remains as a man after God's own heart.

Then there was Peter, one of Jesus's disciples. He swore to Jesus that he would never disown Him,[14] yet when Jesus was arrested and taken to the authorities right before His crucifixion, Peter ran and later denied Him, not just once, but three times.[15] This was a man who had seen Jesus walk on water, who had witnessed with his own eyes the blind receiving sight, the disabled walking, and demons fleeing, yet his fear took over his logic and he denied knowing Jesus.

How often does fear take over your logic and cause you to do something you later regret? It may be fear, or it may be another emotion that takes over, that is too strong for you to think clearly and makes you fall prey to sin. You lie, you steal, you yell, you eat, you drink, or maybe you just isolate yourself. Regardless of how you react and what your struggles are, those moments of weakness do not define you.

Let me come back to Paul for a moment. Earlier I mentioned him grappling with not understanding why he did what he did.[16] He struggled with something he didn't want to do, just like you may be struggling with something you actually hate doing. Yet, he continued to press on in his journey of following Jesus and living out the purpose God had for him, even in his struggles. And don't think he didn't ask God to take away his struggles, because he did. He actually pleaded with God, as 2 Corinthians 12:7-9 records it, "Therefore, in order to keep me from becoming conceited, I was given a thorn in my flesh, a messenger of Satan, to torment me. Three times I pleaded with the Lord to take it away from me. But he said to me, 'My grace is sufficient for you, for my power is made perfect in weakness.' Therefore I will boast all the more gladly about my weaknesses, so that Christ's power may rest on me." What this is saying is that God uses our weaknesses for our own good so that we do not become conceited, and so we will constantly be depending on Him. When we admit our weaknesses, we proclaim the power and goodness of God in our life.

What is your thorn in your flesh right now? What is something you had asked God to take away, yet you keep struggling with? Is it outbursts of anger when you have a bad day? Is it envy or gossip? Is it an addiction to technology, alcohol, drugs, food, or sex? Is it fear, anxiety, or depression? Or maybe control, perfectionism, or self-harm?

At an early age, I became aware of my sexuality and it became my thorn in the flesh. It tormented me and I did not know how to overcome that desire; I was trying to control it, yet I stumbled into it over and over again. I had not understood that God's grace was sufficient for me, especially if it continued to happen after I repented. Because I kept it hidden, it brought shame into my life. The shame produced its consequential effects.

Dr. Brown, in her book *I Thought It Was Just Me*, explains the causes and effects of shame, stating, "Along with many other shame researchers, I've come to the conclusion that shame is much more likely to be the source of destructive behaviors than it is to be the solution. It is human nature to feel affirmed and valued. When we experience shame, we feel disconnected and desperate for belonging and recognition."[17] We have been created for connection, and if exposing shame threatens our connection, we will avoid it at all cost. When Adam and Eve sinned by disobeying God, shame entered into the world. It says in Genesis 3:7-8, "Then the eyes of both of them were opened, and they knew they were naked; so they sewed fig leaves together and made coverings for themselves. Then the man and his wife heard the sound of the Lord God as he was walking in the garden in the cool of the day, and they hid from Lord God among the trees of the garden." Shame makes you want to hide, to cover yourself, because you don't want to be exposed, and appear naked.

In my situation, I did not want my parents to think less of me because I was continuing to do what they told me not to do, so I hid. I felt guilty doing it, and the more I tried not to do it, the worse it got. The guilt produced shame and made me think something was wrong with me. The difference between guilt and shame is that guilt has to do with action—I did something bad—and shame has to do with who you are—I am bad. The problem was, I didn't know what it was and how to stop my actions. I just thought of myself as bad. This feeling of shame reinforced the same behavior even further because it was the exact behavior that helped me escape my emotional turmoil.

Dr. Mark Baker in his book *Overcoming Shame*, states, "Feeling shame makes you feel bad about yourself for being who you are and thus predisposes you to act in bad ways."[18] Moreover, it had created in me a need for control because I couldn't control this aspect of my life. This frustration spilled out as anger, perfectionism, and all-or-nothing behaviors.

Your struggle might be different. You might tell yourself that you have everything under control. I thought I had my struggle under control too. Yet, when I actually admitted it, I knew it was the struggle controlling me. What is important to understand is that sin struggles will be with us for the rest of our lives—as long as we are in this sinful body—but they do not have to be in charge. When Jesus died for us, He took our shame and nailed it to the cross, so we no longer have to be stuck in the cycle of sin and shame because we have a new identity in Him. Romans 10:11 says, "As Scripture says, 'Anyone who believes in him will never be put to shame.'"

What is beautiful is that there is no sin that is too shameful for God. He bore the shame we were supposed to bear, so we can live free from constant feelings of condemnation. Romans 8:1-4 proclaims this truth, "Therefore, there is now no condemnation for those who are in Christ Jesus, because through Christ Jesus the law of the Spirit who gives life has set you free from the law of sin and death. For what the law was powerless to do because it was weakened by the flesh, God did by sending his own Son in the likeness of sinful flesh to be a sin offering. And so he condemned sin in the flesh, in order that the righteous requirement of the law might be fully met in us, who do not live according to the flesh but according to the Spirit." Which is to say that your debt for your sin and the shame associated with that has been paid. You may still turn to your sin, but only because of your weak faith in the work of Jesus. As your faith grows, you will stop turning to your sin.

You see, when you feel shame, you feel like you're worthless, good for nothing, and dirty; you will continue to live up to that expectation because that is who you believe you are. When you start believing that you are priceless, someone who Jesus would die for, a son and daughter of God, you begin living as such.

As a child, I repented multiple times for my sin, but I did not fully grasp how Jesus took my shame and that I was no longer defined by my sin. I was not a *Zamarashka*, but I was a daughter of God, beautiful, holy, priceless. I also did not understand how to live by the Spirit and not according to the flesh, which kept me in my prison of sin—miserable and confused. The understanding that I would still struggle with sin after coming to Christ and not be condemned allowed me to fully embrace the sacrifice He made, which set me free from my feelings of inadequacy.

Christianity is not a works-based religion where one has to labor to clean up their life in order to feel worthy. It is a faith-based religion that produces good works because of Jesus's efforts. This means you can stop believing the lie that you don't sin after coming to Christ and embrace the truth that sin struggles will continue until Jesus takes us home. But know that with each struggle, He will draw you closer and give you the power to overcome as you turn to Him in faith because you no longer have to cover up your shame.

Lie #2:	I will not struggle with sin after coming to Christ.
Truth #2	I will still struggle with sin after coming to Christ.

Before you move on to the next chapter, reflect on the following questions:

1. What are some things you don't want to do, but keep doing anyway?

2. When are you most tempted to engage in those behaviors?

3. What have you done to help yourself control these behaviors?

4. What thoughts go through your mind after you do something you regret?

5. Who does God say that you are in Him?

Chapter 3

New Identity

> "But you are a chosen people, a royal priesthood, a holy nation, God's special possession, that you may declare the praises of him who called you out of darkness into his wonderful light. Once you were not a people, but now you are the people of God; once you had not received mercy, but now you have received mercy."
>
> **— 1 Peter 2:9-10**

When my parents got permission to leave Russia and immigrate to the United States of America, I felt like I was given a chance to start over. On March 20, 1992, at the age of 11, our family packed our livelihood and moved to

America—the so-called *promised land,* flowing with milk and honey, as the Bible describes it.[19] I felt like I was moving to heaven because I had often heard it portrayed as a free country with limitless possibilities. It had always been our dream to move because of the persecution we experienced in Russia, and, even though the communist regime had already ended by that point, this new land promised us opportunities, unlike the limited opportunities in our homeland. In the United States, we could make all our dreams come true.

We settled in Seattle and I started attending school at the end of the fifth grade. I remember our first day as we all stood with signs at the bus station. The signs had our names, which told the school bus driver that we needed to be picked up. It was embarrassing, and I felt stupid as people stared at us as if there was something wrong with us. At school, they gave me a translator, but when he started translating, I didn't understand him either because he spoke Ukrainian. I was too embarrassed to tell him I didn't understand, so I just stayed confused. It was not an easy transition.

In the middle of sixth grade, my family moved to another house, and I went from elementary to middle school because the school I was to attend had sixth grade in middle school. I was wearing hand-me-downs because we didn't have a lot of money to purchase clothes, and I also could not speak English very well. I did make a few friends there, but the majority of the time, I was ridiculed for my clothes and my name. My full Russian name is Ol'ga, with a soft *l,* but in English it was Olga. There were so many ways to vary a name in Russian—like

Olechka, Olushka, Olya, Olenka—and my family had called me Olushka ever since my ninth birthday when a family friend wrote a poem, "Olushka, you are nine years old today, with so many happy years ahead." Except in Russian, it was a six-stanza rhyming poem, and my family teased me with this line, *"Олюшка, тебе сегодня девять, сколько лет счастливых впереди?"* I begrudged the poem and tossed it in the trash, but the first line remained with me forever. Now, as I write this book exactly thirty years later, I can attest that this family friend was right. But let me not get ahead of myself. What I was saying was that there were so many ways to say my name but in English, people didn't pronounce it right more often than not.

I remember a group of girls bullying me, and though I didn't understand what they were saying, I knew it was mean. They ridiculed my name and instead of saying Olga, they called me Ogre. I didn't know what it meant so I didn't pay much attention to it, but when I learned the definition, I started to resent my name. I was nowhere near being a monster nor a giant who feeds on human flesh, as the definition read, and I wondered, *How could someone call me that?* I became hesitant to tell people my name. I wanted to be someone else.

I heard other people saying how they liked going by another name, and I wondered, *Could I do that?* One of my friends named Kolya, or full name Nikolai, called himself Nick. I started thinking that my name was probably translated to Nicole, since Kolya was made up of *K* and *Olya* and my name in Russian was Olya, meaning my English name had to be Nicole. At least that was the reasoning that went through my thirteen-year-old head. But I wondered, *How can I just start telling people that I want to go by Nicole? How can I just be this new person?*

Fortunately, at the start of my eighth-grade year, my family received government housing help and we were able to move to a home in a different neighborhood. This was a dream house, with a view outlooking the Puget Sound. I transferred to a junior high school and had an opportunity to start fresh. This was going to be my chance to start my new life, but not only was I afraid to take that step, I also didn't know how.

When my mom took me to the school for registration, they asked my name and as Mom pronounced it, a flood of memories consumed me. I remembered how rejected I felt, how embarrassed of my outfits, my broken English, and of my ugly name. I hated being *Olga*. Without even thinking, with undoubtful confidence I corrected her, "I would like to go by Nicole." The office lady immediately wrote in *Nicole* and this marked the beginning of a whole new life for me.

When I first stepped on campus, I could not believe how different people treated me. I had picked up a few more words in English, which gave me more confidence in casual conversations. I had also taken off the hand-me-downs and put on more trendy clothes. I also made my hair resemble the styles at school. I was ready to begin my new life as Nicole. The first few days, when people called my name, it would take me a moment to realize they were talking to me. But eventually I got used to it. I made friends with the coolest girls on campus and only told them I was Russian when I found it convenient—after I'd earned their acceptance.

I was a new person and my life was going in the right direction. I started to try hard in school because I was able to understand more English. I went above and beyond in everything I put my mind to. I was the fastest girl typist in the entire school, and the second fastest runner in track. I had the highest geometry grade in ninth grade; it was 99.9%. I still have that paper that my teacher posted on the wall. She decided to give it to me for a keepsake because I was at the top of the class. I was getting certificate after certificate in everything possible—I was excelling, and I loved it.

Success seemed to fall in my lap as I started living in my new identity. This *promised land* seemed very promising, and I felt good about who I had become. I looked forward to graduating from junior high and going to high school. My dreams could become reality after all.

The only problem with all of my success and living in my new identity was that I knew I could lose it all in an instant. If I didn't keep up my appearance of looking like an American girl, I would be rejected. If I told people my real name, I might be seen differently. If I stopped being the best in everything, I would not be noticed. Everything I had depended on my effort and strength, so I had to keep being good, being likable, being like people expected me to be in order to be accepted. I had to earn it. I had to earn the *promised land* to drink the milk and honey it provided. Though I found that I actually had to make

57

the milk and honey: I changed my name, changed how I looked, changed how I talked, and changed friends. Even Russian people thought I was American for some time. I worked really hard to be accepted.

Many of us go through life trying to earn everything we have. This country demands we work hard. Everything is achieved through effort and hard work. And there is nothing wrong with that. However, when it comes to our salvation, we cannot earn it or keep it with our efforts. Thus, if we take this mentality into our understanding about God, we will live a miserable life, filled with a constant search for approval; a life where nothing we do is ever enough, and everything we achieve is worthless in the eyes of eternity. Ephesians 1:4 says, "For he chose us in him before the creation of the world to be holy and blameless in his sight." Pay close attention to what this verse says. "He chose us in him before the creation of the world to be holy and blameless." There is *nothing* you can to do to make yourself righteous, you already *are* in Him.

It says in Romans 3:23, "All have sinned and fall short of the glory of God." *All* means *all*. There is not one person who hasn't sinned and not one person who can completely stop sinning while on this side of heaven. We cannot do anything to be accepted into God's family because we have all messed up. Every one of us is born a sinner, whether we can admit that or not.

We often compare ourselves to others to feel better about ourselves or judge others for their sins, which we see as bigger than our own. But what we don't understand is that when we point one finger toward someone else, there are three other fingers pointing back at us. Romans 2:1 says, "You, therefore, have no excuse, you who pass judgment on someone else, for at whatever point you judge another, you are condemning yourself, because you who pass judgment do the same things." This is a sobering verse for me. When I am appalled about someone else's sin, thinking *I would have never done that*, I am condemning myself. I am no better than the person who sinned. I might sin differently, but I still sin. However, the good news is that Jesus had conquered sin and you are no longer in debt for your sin if you can accept this truth. In other words, sin has no power over you because it's canceled.

It will still show up in your life, as we discussed in the previous chapter, because you live in a sinful body, but it does not define you. You are defined by a new name. Do you believe that? Isaiah 62:12 talks about the restoration of Zion, the holy city, God's chosen people, and says, "They will be called the Holy People, the Redeemed of the Lord; and you will be called Sought After, the City No Longer Deserted." Isn't this beautiful? Did you know this is about you? You are chosen by Him to be His holy people; cared for and redeemed, not deserted.

You know how amazing it feels to be chosen? I remember when I applied for the vice principal pool in my district, and went through the interview process, which was all on its own stressful and long with multiple levels, and then waited for the outcome. Finally, when I received the long-awaited email, it read, "You have been chosen to be in the VP pool." I was chosen out of seventy-five applicants. They chose me, and probably a few others too, but that didn't matter. And it was just a pool, which meant nothing because I still had to interview for a specific school, but still, it felt good to be chosen.

These words speak life into us. Who doesn't like to be chosen? It means that you have something better to offer than others. It means that you somehow have earned it. And in my case for the job interview, it meant *yes;* I had earned it based on my answers and my experience. But not in the case of Jesus; He chose you only because He loves you. Ephesians 2:4-5, "But because of his great love for us, God, who is rich in mercy, made us alive with Christ even when we were dead in transgressions—it is by grace you have been saved." Basically, He loved us in our sins and saved us by grace, not because we have done anything right.

He died on the cross for us purely out of love, which means He accepts you just as you are. He knew what He was getting before He created you—your mistakes, your ugly sins, your secrets, all the things you were going to do that you yourself were going to regret. He saw it all, and He chose you anyway. You don't have to look different, talk different, or behave different when you come to Him. I felt I had to do that to fit into my new identity of being Nicole; Nicole had to look American, talk American, and behave like an American. But we don't have to do that for God. He does it Himself as we submit and follow His lead.

I work with teachers and we often talk about how our behavior directly stems from our belief system. For example, if I believe I am capable of running five miles, I will most likely do it. But if I believe I am not capable, I probably will never run, nor even try. Or, if I believe I am smart, I will look for ways to solve a problem, I will be able to speak confidently, I will feel like I have something to contribute, and I will be able to experience success. If I believe I am stupid, I will probably not try solving a problem, I will be hesitant to speak, I will feel I have nothing to contribute, and I will experience failure. My belief about myself drives my behavior.

These beliefs come from messages we receive growing up, from family and friends, or even teachers and authority figures, and they shape our identity. If we grew up in an environment that supported our belief that we are valued and capable of success, we will have a high self-efficacy. However, if it was the opposite, then we grow up thinking we are incapable and insignificant, leading us on a path of unsuccessful lives. Kim, John R. Baldwin, and Thomas Ewald (2006) conducted a study on the relationship between shame, guilt, and self-efficacy and found that people who experienced more shame had a lower sense of self-efficacy, meaning that they did not believe they were capable of success.[20] Thus, high levels of shame lead to low levels of self-worth, translating into low self-efficacy, which potentially leads a person down the path of self-soothing or using coping behaviors such as eating, drinking, smoking, isolating, or drug use. The authors state, "Shame and self-efficacy are at the foundation of a person's choices and reactions."[21] According to this research, what we believe about ourselves will directly translate into our behavior.

However, it takes a great deal of effort to maintain high self-efficacy and believe in yourself on your own because your belief is based on your past success. But with God, even without past success, you can have a high self-efficacy (what you believe about yourself) because of His success, which takes away all the pressure of you relying on self and allows you to rely on an all-powerful, all-capable, and all-perfect God. He has taken care of your shame and failure on the cross, which gives you the highest scale of self-efficacy you can ever have, not because of your ability, but because of His. And because of this, you no longer have to make choices or react based on your faulty beliefs about yourself. Instead, you can act and behave according to your new identity in your God-given purpose. Ephesians 2:10 states, "For we are God's workmanship, created in Christ Jesus to do good works, which God prepared in advance for us to do."

This is where faith in Jesus and understanding of our new identity in Him can transform our life. Regardless of what environment you come from, what messages you received, you will not live out your true identity unless you know who you were created to be. There is a God who says you are valued, capable, accepted, and loved more than anything in this world and He has a purpose for your life now and in eternity. You don't have to work or do anything to deserve this calling, except believe in His Son Jesus.

Just like when I got my new identity as Nicole and I felt like sky was the limit. I was motivated to be the best I could be in everything I put my mind to. When we know our true identity in Christ, that motivates us to be the best we can be, and it takes our attention away from being self-absorbed to instead focusing on others. However, at that time, my identity was based on my appearance to the world. I cared about what others thought about me based on how I looked and how I behaved. It was rooted in people-pleasing and in the things I had. If people had found out that I was not really "Nicole" and instead knew me as a Russian girl who didn't understand English very well and relied on government aid, I would have lost my identity.

Not so with God. People can let us down, but not God. With my change of identity, I had to do the work to earn acceptance from people. When we accept our new identity in Christ, He takes us through a process called sanctification, which simply means to make us more like Him. You do not have to do it yourself, but if you follow His lead, He will do it. As you allow this process to take place, He will transform you from the inside out. It is not an external process of changing behavior, but an internal process of transforming the heart. It is much more beautiful, freeing, and life-giving than trying to fix yourself. And it begins with you believing who you are in Christ.

Are you trying to find your identity in people, like I did? Or maybe it's career? Children? Family? Significant other? Possessions? Because I can tell you, it will wear you out. But if you put your faith in Jesus and believe that He has paid the price to give you a new identity, where you are no longer defined by your choices, but rather by His perfection, then you will experience peace and rest. There is nothing you need to do to keep up appearances because God accepts you and loves you simply because you are His child.

In retrospect, my early teens were spent trying to find identity in all the wrong things. I thought I found myself in my new name, but what I failed to realize was that I already had a new identity in Christ. This profound understanding would have helped solve my problem with how people treated me and how I treated myself. You see, having a new name had not changed the way I saw myself. I still felt like someone who did not live up to her own expectations, who struggled with guilt and shame, and who did not have worth. My failure to see myself as Christ saw me did not allow for my heart to change as I continued struggling in my sinful patterns. If I had claimed my new identity then, I would have saved myself much grief, because the only way we can ever be free of our sins and live on purpose is by accepting our new identity in Christ instead of trying to earn it. So my message to you is this: stop believing the lie that you need to do something to earn acceptance and embrace the truth that you are enough.

Lie #3:	There are things I need to do to earn acceptance from God.
Truth #3:	**There is nothing I need to do to earn acceptance from God.**

Before you move into the next chapter, reflect on the following questions:

1. What are some things that you do to earn acceptance from people?

2. What are some things that you do to earn acceptance from God?

3. How does the idea that there is nothing you can do to earn acceptance from God affect you?

4. Read 1 Peter 2:9-10 again. Meditate on this verse and write about who you are in Christ.

Chapter 4

Two Paths

> *"But if we walk in the light, as he is in the light, we have fellowship with one another, and the blood of Jesus, his Son purifies us from all sin. If we claim to be without sin, we deceive ourselves and the truth is not in us. If we confess our sins, he is faithful and just and will forgive us our sins and purify us from all unrighteousness. If we claim we have not sinned, we make him out to be a liar and his word is not in us."*
>
> **— 1 John 1:7-10**

From the time my family moved to America, we had always attended two churches. My parents were members of a Russian church, but in order to learn English quicker, we also attended an American church. As part of this church, my siblings and I would often go to camps with the American youth, and I would see this different church culture that was very interesting to me. They did not have strict rules on how to dress or behave, making it so easy to be around them since I didn't have to worry about how I was dressed or how I behaved, and they constantly smiled. Somehow when people smiled, it made me feel welcomed and at ease. I remember vividly how the pastor of the American church we went to smiled as he greeted everyone at the end of the service. I was so intrigued by how friendly he was, calling me *smiley* because I just couldn't stop smiling. It was so different from what I was used to in my church, where smiling was not appropriate, at least during services. It probably had to do with our culture too, where it was not a custom to smile. Thus, I enjoyed these people and their joyful personalities, partly because they reminded me of my grandfather's smile. However, though no one ever said so directly, the underlying message I had always understood was that American churches were not holding on to the truth as they had a relaxed understanding of the gospel.

The Russian service we attended was a lot like the church I left in Russia. It was made up of immigrants like us, who came from Russia or Ukraine. The church structure was similar, the choir and the preaching the same. There were some exceptions though. It was acceptable for women to put makeup on, wear jewelry, and to cut or color their hair, and not everyone wore head coverings. It was a bit confusing as to why these things were all of a sudden acceptable here, but I did not question it because, in a way, I never really understood why we focus so much on appearance when Jesus focuses on our hearts.

However, we later moved to another larger Russian church because it provided many opportunities for children and youth. This church had stricter rules around dress code. Short skirts and pants were not allowed in church for women or girls, married women had to wear head coverings, and jewelry was prohibited all together. Men were supposed to wear dress pants and dress shirts to services, and if you were to go on stage, a suit and tie were appropriate. Even if you wore pants and jewelry during the week, you could not come to church like that. For me, walking into church was intimidating because I knew people were evaluating my outfit to make sure I was dressed appropriately, ensuring that everyone looked presentable for God in God's house.

I was used to it since this was how I grew up, but after experiencing American church and even a Russian church with less stringent rules, I started to criticize the rules, though not explicitly. Personally, it was an obstacle for attending church because I was more concerned about what I was wearing than about anything else. When I started driving, I often went to the mall to find a new outfit to wear right before church. Also, it cultivated a hypocritical mentality, where I would look one way in church but could look different after. Usually, if this argument ever came up, it was solved by saying that if we comply with rules at work, why not comply with rules at church? Thus, I tried not to question the rules, which shaped the idea that to be accepted as a Christian, I had to look and act a certain way.

When I was fourteen, I went to a youth conference in Portland, Oregon. I remember feeling so grown up being accepted into youth. The church was filled with young people from all over Washington and Oregon. These conferences were a common occurrence in the 1990s in America because Slavic churches tried to stick together in this new country, so they would bring youth from nearby cities for worship, Bible study, and fellowship. Of course, fellowship and the sports after church were what most youth looked forward to. It was an opportunity to socialize, make new friends, and, for some, even an opportunity to meet their future spouse.

I was there to listen to what God had prepared for me. I sat closer to the front and was focused on the message. I can't remember exactly what the message was about, but it again struck my heart and convicted me of my sin. This was something that happened to me often, though some days more than others, and I felt a powerful push to come out and repent. I pushed back because of thoughts that I have done this before, and nothing had changed. I was still sinning no matter how many times I swore to never sin again.

Then I thought that maybe it didn't work because I was too young and didn't understand something or was too weak to control myself when it came to temptation. Maybe this time, if I repented, I'd forever be changed, as I had heard many people say when they repented, they were a new person and never went back to their old ways. I imagined how wonderful that would be, being a new person, being perfect and holy.

Propelled by my enormous desire to be free from sin, guilt, and shame, I rushed to the front of the church, fell on my knees, and cried out to God, asking Him to take away all my sins. I so wanted to be free from sin, free from stumbling, free from going back to the things I didn't want to do. I wanted to be perfect, to live perfect, and, most importantly be loved and accepted by God and others.

When I got up from my knees, I felt like I was in heaven. I felt so light, so free, so new. I felt the guilt and shame flee from me and a renewed spirit enter, yet again.

After service, instead of going to play sports and hanging out, many of the youth decided to go to downtown Portland and evangelize. My heart rejoiced as I walked the streets talking to people about how amazing God is, how He forgives sin, and how He loves people. However, I was a little scared to go to bed that night, knowing tomorrow will be another day to live perfect. Today was easy, I was with people, I was doing God's work, and there was no way I could sin. *But tomorrow?* I questioned myself. *What if I'm alone and temptation comes and I'm not able to resist? What if I fail?*

The fear of failure overwhelmed me. *How can I make sure I never sin again? Is that even possible? Will God still love me?* As I was sharing the gospel with strangers, I could not help but fear my failure. I did not trust myself to never sin again. *What is so good about the gospel anyway? If I have to work so hard to be perfect to remain in God's love, is it really that great of news?*

Coming home that night had me feeling disappointed because all of the high emotions were gone, and I was back to regular life. Oh how I wished God would just take me to heaven after I repented so I'd be perfectly clean for Him, washed in His blood. I knew I was going to make a mess again. I knew I wasn't able to be perfect. I had tried so many times and I had always failed—always! And what do you know? I failed this time again. My failure brought the verse from Hebrews 10:26-27 to drum in my head, "If we deliberately keep on sinning after we have received the knowledge of the truth, no sacrifice for sins is left, but only a fearful expectation of judgment and of raging fire that will consume the enemies of God." I was convinced I was not supposed to sin, yet I still sinned. It was not deliberate, but it always happened.

And did I try not to sin? All the time! I'd wake up in the morning and tell myself, "Today I will be perfect." Then, I'd be pretty good while nothing tempted me or bothered me, but as soon as something would, I'd fail again. I'd get upset with my siblings, I'd say some mean things, and then isolate myself in my room. *Does that mean I have no more sacrifice left? Does that mean His blood only washed away some sins, and not others? Did He only forgive me when I begged Him to forgive and if I slip again, I should prepare for judgment and the punishment of hell? Does my salvation depend on my ability to be perfect? Does it depend on my ability to ask for forgiveness? Can I just ask ahead of time because I know I'll mess up in the future?*

All these questions did not allow me to live in freedom. I thought I had limited atonement for my sin. I thought I lost salvation every time I sinned, and I had to repent in church again. Or maybe I needed to try harder, pray more, read more Bible. What a miserable life in Christ.

Nonetheless, I started to be really serious about reading and praying daily, not that I wasn't before, but I thought maybe I just needed to make sure to read the whole Bible. Starting again in Genesis, I read trying to not miss a word. I even read every genealogy and tried to pronounce every name, thinking that if I had skipped something, I'd miss a really important truth. I would have a perfect record of reading daily until a busy day when I'd fail. Then, I would get upset and stop reading altogether for a while until I felt guilty. Once guilt set in, I'd start again in Genesis. Sometimes I'd skip the middle of the Bible and go straight to the New Testament, remembering my grandpa's advice to just focus on the Gospels if we did not understand the Old Testament.

I loved reading stories about Jesus and how He brought healing to people, opened the eyes of the blind, raised people from the dead, stood up for the woman who committed adultery, talked to the woman at the well, delivered people from evil spirits, and on and on and on. I wanted Jesus to perform a miracle on me. *If He did all that for those people, why can't He make me stop sinning? Why can't I live free from this constant feeling of guilt and shame, constant feeling of failure, and constant desire and inability to be perfect?*

73

I kept turning to my only solution for my brokenness—doing more. I attended every Bible study, every choir practice, every church meeting. I attended multiple services: first going to an American church with Sunday school classes, then Russian service, and then youth service in the evening. I volunteered in Russian school and Sunday school. I was very involved in church. However, nothing in my spiritual life changed. At least, I didn't feel that I had stopped sinning like I thought I was supposed to. I had a few perfect days, or so I thought. I even felt like I had perfect weeks, but eventually, I'd fail. I'd try again and fail again.

What a failure I am.

I was a sinner trying to reach perfection through my own efforts, trying to work on my sin. From an outside perspective I looked like I was a good Christian girl. You might say I produced fruit of repentance. Though inside I was struggling, broken, and completely discouraged and worn out from trying to be perfect. I remember one day I came home from church only to hear that someone made a comment in church about the length of my skirt. What was disheartening for me was that people didn't care about what was going on inside my heart, people only saw the external work and appearance.

Have you ever attempted to stop sinning by trying? You told yourself, *I need to stop yelling at my kids,* and that same day you yelled at them even harder? Or you told yourself *I will stop gossiping,* and the next thing you know you are in the middle of a heated conversation about someone and you can't seem to walk away? How about trying to lose weight? As soon as you focus on your weight, instead of losing, you somehow gain more pounds. It seems like the more you focus on trying not to do something, the more you do it. You can definitely try to be better, try to yell less, gossip less, or eat less, but the problem is not yelling, gossiping, or eating. The problem is sin. It's like a chronic disease, a curse. And the more you focus on it, the more it controls you.

Growing up I often heard you have to choose the road you want to travel, either take the road of destruction and choose sin, or take the road of righteousness and never sin. Of course, I wanted to take the road of righteousness, but I kept on sinning. Did that mean I was on the road of destruction? This misunderstanding came from Matthew 7:13-14, where Jesus talks about narrow and wide gates, "Enter through the narrow gate. For wide is the gate and broad is the road that leads to destruction, and many enter through it. But small is the gate and narrow the road that leads to life, and only a few find it." When you read this, you probably think it is talking about the wicked people, the sinners, who enter through the wide gate as it's the easy thing to do. You probably think, *But I am choosing the narrow gate, I beat myself up for sinning and I try really hard not to sin. I am not evil like those people who choose sin. I'm better. I go to church, I sing on a worship team, I lead a Bible study group, I read the Bible and pray every day. I believe in Jesus. I am sure I'm entering through the narrow gate.*

But did you ever stop to think that you and I could also be entering through the wide gate by relying on our own works to keep our salvation, which is no different than the rest of the world's religions, or even the irreligious? If you think you can do something to lose the salvation you never earned, you need to reflect on your faith. 2 Corinthians 13:5 says, "Examine yourselves to see whether you are in the faith; test yourselves." We could be in the same boat as the wicked people who choose the road of destruction. In God's eyes, when we fail to trust the work of Jesus, all our righteous acts are like filthy rags.[22] You might say, "Does that mean I won't lose salvation when I sin?" Well, first answer this question. Are you able not to sin? The answer is *no*. So to say that when you sin you will lose salvation would be to say that Jesus died for nothing because none of us are sinless. The debt for your sin has been paid on the cross—you owe nothing. What do you want to do now? Do you want to go sin? I doubt you do if you consider yourself a Christian because you know how destructive sin is and how much pain it cost Jesus. Why would you want to live in it? This is exactly what Apostle Paul says in Romans 6:1-2, "What shall we say, then? Shall we go on sinning so that grace may increase? By no means! We are those who died to sin; how can we live in it any longer?" It doesn't mean you won't sin, but you do not want to go on sinning, if you understand this truth. I didn't want to sin, but my lack of understanding of the gospel kept me in my sin and shame because I had not surrendered it to Him and did not yet believe that He indeed paid for all of it.

Also, if you read the verses that follow Romans 6:1-2, you will see that Jesus talks about false prophets who do not bear good fruit. These passages conclude with Jesus saying that He never knew them, even though they did all those things like prophesy, drive out demons, and perform miracles.[23] This is what happens when we live by our own efforts, like I did growing up. We produce no good fruit and Jesus doesn't know us because we have not believed in the work He did on the cross, but instead relied on our own work.

I recently came across a book called *The Cure,* by John Lynch, Bruce McNicol, and Bill Thrall, which resonated with me. It provides a vivid description of two paths, somewhat similar to the idea of the narrow and wide gates in the Bible. One path is Pleasing God and the other is Trusting God. The path that pleases God leads to a Room with Good Intentions and the one that trusts God leads to a Room of Grace. The Room of Good Intentions is full of beautiful, flawless people striving hard to be perfect and sinless, yet feeling weary and fake. The Room of Grace is full of people trusting God with their sin, living out who God says they are. In the first room, people work on their sin to achieve an intimate relationship with God. In the second room, people have an intimate relationship with God because their sin is paid for on the cross. In the first room, people hide their struggles due to fear of being judged and unmasked, while in the second room, everyone admits their struggles with no judgment as no masks exist.[24]

If you are trying to stop sinning by good intentions, you might be on a path of pleasing God instead of trusting God by faith. You probably feel like this when it comes to sin: "Despite all my passionate sincerity, I keep sinning. Then I get frustrated on trying not to sin. Then it all repeats: Same sin, same thoughts, same failure."[25] This sounds exactly like my experience. And the worst part was that I thought I was the only one because nobody else ever talked about their sin struggles. All the Christian people I knew looked perfect, talked perfect, lived perfect—at least that was my impression. But it was tiring because I constantly had to keep up appearances, and I could never be real or honest, which made everything feel superficial and fake. The sentiment of never feeling like I measured up was constant and no matter how hard I tried not to sin, I kept sinning. Because there is only one way we can please God, and that is with our faith, as we read in Hebrews 11:6, "And without faith it is impossible to please God." Galatians 5:4 also says, "You who are trying to be justified by law have been alienated from Christ; you have fallen away from grace." I never measured up because I could never justify myself by my own work.

There is also a verse in 1 John 1:7 that added more fire to this uneasy feeling of never measuring up. It says, "But if we walk in the light, as he is in the light, we have fellowship with one another, and the blood of Jesus, his Son, purifies us from all sin." I thought walking in the light meant you don't sin, that if you keep on sinning, the blood will no longer purify you. It only purifies you when you walk in the light. This was confusing because why would you need the blood to purify you if you don't sin?

The following verses provide more insight. "If we claim to be without sin, we deceive ourselves and the truth is not in us. If we confess our sins, he is faithful and just and will forgive us our sins and purify us from all unrighteousness. If we claim we have not sinned, we make him out to be a liar and his word has no place in our lives," (1 John 1:9-10). So walking in the light does not mean that we do not sin, but rather that we do sin and we confess that sin. By confessing sin and walking away from it with God's truth, we live in the light. Ha! That's amazing news!

But how do we confess sin in a community where nobody sins? Or at least where it is the impression that nobody sins. Everyone is so concerned about trying not to sin, that to admit one has sinned could mean being labeled as a sinner and face ex-communication. And nobody wants that to happen to them. So people either hide their sin, or regard some sins as acceptable (maybe the ones they think don't lead to death).[26] I will not go into this concept of different sins, but it is a mentality that can lead to an incorrect view of sin. *Could this be why I have not heard anyone struggle with sin?* But God is holy, and every sin is rebellion; the sins that lead to death and the ones that don't are all still sins. Gossip, outbursts of anger, slander, and bitterness are all sins that may not lead to physical death, but they are still destructive. By confessing these, we can expose them, and live in the light. Ephesians 5:8-10 says, "For you were once darkness, but now you are light in the Lord. Live as children of light (for the fruit of the light consists in all goodness, righteousness and truth) and find out what pleases the Lord." When we are honest about our sins and struggles with each other, we encourage each other in the faith, and faith is what pleases the Lord.

When we as a church become hyper-focused on behavior and appearance, it prevents people from being able to confess and expose sin, which promotes a work-based mentality where people have a skewed view of sin. This type of environment breeds hypocrisy, penetrating deep into the heart of every member of the church. No wonder Jesus warned us to be on guard against the yeast of the Pharisees and Sadducees in Mathew 16:6,[27] because their teaching promoted a work-based salvation.

Unfortunately, this hypocrite mentality was nothing new to me since I had seen it from childhood, and it seemed normal. It penetrated every aspect of my life and the lives of the people around me. I was shocked to learn a family friend committed adultery, while I watched an R-rated movie. I judged smokers and drunks yet overate at a buffet after church. I was appalled how someone couldn't quit drugs, while I couldn't quit yelling or gossiping. It is so easy to be a hypocrite; one doesn't even need to try. We often judge others while doing the same ourselves. Yes, our sins might look different, but nonetheless they were sins. Matthew records Jesus's words in Chapter 23:27-28, "Woe to you, teachers of the law and Pharisees, you hypocrites! You are like whitewashed tombs, which look beautiful on the outside but on the inside are full of the bones of the dead and everything unclean. In the same way, on the outside you appear to people as righteous but on the inside you are full of hypocrisy and wickedness." These people looked beautiful, they dressed up for God, but inside they were evil, why? Because they put their faith in themselves and their works, not in the work of Jesus.

Jesus actually pronounces seven woes on these teachers of the law and Pharisees. The first of these woes is recorded in Matthew 23:13, "Woe to you teachers of the law and Pharisees, you hypocrites! You shut the door of the kingdom of heaven in people's faces. You yourselves do not enter, nor will you let those enter who are trying to." Jesus was brutal with these people. He was basically saying that instead of leading people to God, they were shutting them out. They were the leaders of the Room with Good Intentions, the wide gate, which seemed like the narrow gate because of the hard work it took.

But Jesus came to show the path to the other room, the Room of Grace, the narrow gate, which can be found by trusting God, rather than by trying to please Him with good works. And you might think that trusting God sounds too easy. Maybe for someone who already lost all control and hope, but for people like me, who grew up in a Christian family, it's not that easy. It is easier to rely on what you know, on what you can control, on what is familiar—ourselves. But trusting requires letting go of our control, letting go of our pride, letting go of what's familiar, and trusting God with our sin, with our work, and with our life. This is why Jesus said in Matthew 21:31, "Truly I tell you, the tax collectors and the prostitutes are entering the kingdom of God ahead of you." They accepted the work of Jesus on the cross for their sin knowing they could not save themselves. But the Pharisees were certain they could do it by their works, their pride and control getting in the way

81

of their salvation. This was why I could not live by faith because I relied on my own efforts with my pride getting in the way.

I encounter many people nowadays who left church because of their frustrations with the unreasonable expectations set on them, or others who felt out of place because they looked different than the norm. They were worn out from continually trying and never being good enough. These people had left because they could not grow spiritually due to a lack of understanding of the full gospel. Some of these people found other churches that accepted them and lead them to the truth, while others never returned to church.

I don't know what your experience is when it comes to church. But what I do know is that any Christian church can have people in both camps—those who put their faith in Jesus and those who heavily rely on their own work. The important part is to evaluate the teaching. In a faith-based teaching church, the focus is on what Jesus had done on the cross to reconcile us to Himself by grace through faith. This faith produces fruit described in the book of James:[28] taking care of orphans and widows, not discriminating people, and loving others. People feel accepted and loved in this type of church. In a work-based teaching church, the focus is on rule following and external appearance. People feel judged, shamed, discouraged, and weary in this type of church. I am certain churches do not do so intentionally and culture could also play a role here, but it is still important for every church to evaluate its practices and repent of unintentionally promoting work-based salvation.

Why? Because when Jesus fulfilled the law, He made us ministers of a new covenant that is not based on the law, but on the work of Jesus, who as a matter of fact, fulfilled the whole law. Second Corinthians 3:6 says, "He has made us competent as ministers of a new covenant—not of the letter but of the Spirit; for the letter kills, but the Spirit gives life." Since Jesus fulfilled the law, we who put our faith in Him, have also fulfilled the requirements of the law, simply by faith. Now, instead of focusing on rule following, we must focus on growing up in our faith and our understanding of who we are in Christ.

This is important because if we focus on rules and external appearance, we are going to be living under the old covenant of the law, which kills. The reason it kills is because it does not allow us to follow the lead of the Spirit and grow in an intimate relationship with Jesus. Remember how many times Jesus broke the Jewish law? He touched the dead and unclean people when he was not supposed to. He broke the Sabbath, which was against the law and he could have been put to death for that, but he did it to bring people healing and hope. The Bible records multiple occasions when Pharisees were out to kill Jesus because he had done something that conflicted with their rules. The same thing happens when we set up rules that prevent people from coming to Christ. If we give a person a list of rules to follow when they receive Jesus, we are basically telling them to trust in those rules rather than the work of Jesus, and inadvertently rob them of the good news of the gospel.

This is not to say that the problem is with the law, because God is a God of order and he requires absolute perfection. Hence, this is why Jesus had to die so we could be made perfect, without having to fulfill all the requirements of the law. The law was given to lead us to Christ as Galatians 3:24 says, "So the law was our guardian until Christ came that we might be justified by faith." What this is saying is that the law was given so we can understand our state of depravity. Romans 7:7-8 says, "For I would not have known what coveting really was if the law had not said, 'You shall not covet.' But sin, seizing the opportunity afforded by the commandment, produced in me every kind of coveting. For apart from the law, sin was dead." Let me put it in terms we can all understand. It's like telling yourself you will go on a diet by restricting sweets. You made a rule for yourself. All of a sudden, all you want to eat is sweets. Why? Because creating a rule for what not to have makes you want it more. Without the rule, there is no desire. Living by the Spirit is like living without dietary rules, the desires and cravings go away. This is why when we give a new believer a list of rules to follow after coming to Christ, we are making a dwelling for sin to continue its destructive cycle. As Galatians 3:10 puts it, "For all who rely on the works of the law are under a curse, as it is written: 'Cursed is everyone who does not continue to do everything written in the Book of the Law.'" Instead, what we have to do is teach about the truth of the gospel, which has the power to heal the person from this destructive curse of sin, leading them to a transformation from the inside out, rather than from the outside in.

We are under the law of Christ, as we read in Galatians 5:13-14, "You, my brothers and sisters, were called to be free. But do not use your freedom to indulge the flesh; rather, serve one another humbly in love. For the entire law is fulfilled in keeping this one command: 'Love your neighbor as yourself.'" It also says in Galatians 6:2 to "Carry each other's burdens, and in this way you will fulfill the law of Christ." In other words, our concentration should go from focusing on ourselves, to focusing on loving God and loving others.

This truth is not new to me and I am sure not new to you, either, but because I was so focused on my own justification of being accepted, I was not capable of loving others the way Christ wanted me to. As fifteen-year-old Nicole, I was desperately trying to fulfill the law by being perfect, but I was failing, which only brought more guilt, shame, and hiding, then repeating the cycle again and again. The cycle of sin loses its power when we understand that we are not going to lose salvation when we sin. Now we can be free to confess the sin that still entangles us, allow our church family to pray for us, and encourage us to walk by faith.

I hope that by understanding this truth, you will be able to finally come to Jesus and release the heavy burden you've been carrying all your life—trying to be good in your own strength. I also hope you will be able to be more authentic and real with people by confessing your sin and allowing the blood of Jesus to cleanse you, because this will lead to a deeper fellowship with the people you do life with. I love the verses from Matthew 11:28-30, "Come to me, all you who are weary and burdened, and I will give you rest. Take my yoke upon you and learn from me, for I am gentle and humble in heart, and you will find rest for your souls. For my yoke is easy and my burden is light." Jesus desires to take your heavy burden so you can find rest. Will you let Him?

If you are tired of living a superficial life in the Room of Good Intentions, the Room of Grace is still available. There, you can come as you are, with all your issues, struggles, and sins. There, you will find many more people just like you, sinners in need of a Savior who are made perfect in Christ; people who rely only on the work of Jesus instead of their own work. And the best part is, they can now focus on their God-given purpose, as we read in Ephesians 2:8-10, "For it is by grace you have been saved, through faith—and this not from yourselves, it is the gift of God—not by works, so that no one can boast. For we are God's workmanship, created in Christ Jesus to do good works, which God prepared in advance for us to do." This good work is not to appease God, but rather to accomplish the purpose He created you for, which is to love Him and love people. So stop obsessing over your sin and obsess over Jesus, who paid for your sin to give you a life of freedom, walking in the light and living on purpose by faith.

Lie #4:	I work on my sin so I can grow in my relationship with God and others.
Truth #4:	**I confess my sin so I can grow in my relationship with God and others.**

Before you move into the next chapter, reflect on the following questions:

1. What path are you on? Are you trying to please God or trust God?

2. What are some sins you keep working on?

3. What are rules you set for yourself, besides loving God and loving people, that may be interfering with you living by faith?

4. How do you feel about confessing sin to another person?

5. How would you feel and react if someone confessed a sin to you?

Chapter 5

Pursuit of Happiness

> *"'For I know the plans I have for you,' declares the Lord, 'plans to prosper you and not to harm you, plans to give you a hope and a future. Then you will call on me and come and pray to me, and I will listen to you. You will seek me and find me when you seek me with all your heart.'"*
>
> **— Jeremiah 29:11-13**

Growing up, I never really understood how people find their spouses. My parents didn't share many details about how they met or about how they knew they were meant to be together. All I knew was that my dad liked my mom when she was six and he was twelve. Their parents knew each other and often helped each other out when the water would be shut off, which happened often in the Soviet Union. My mom's family went to my dad's family to take showers when their water wasn't available, and vice versa. One of those times when my mom was over at my dad's, my dad told himself that he was going to marry her. As they got older, he went to the army, she waited from him, they wrote letters back and forth, and when he returned, they got married. Sweet and simple. How hard could it be?

Not so simple for me. First of all, I didn't like any boys when I was little until my friends in first grade asked me if I had a crush on someone. I was too embarrassed to tell them I didn't, so I picked the cutest guy in my class and said I liked him. After that, the more I thought about it, the more I started paying attention to boys, but I wasn't sure what I was supposed to like. Maybe their cute haircut or the shape of their eyes? I was actually making myself find something that I liked about boys. I seemed to gravitate toward dark-haired ones though. I always said I would have a husband who was tall, dark, and handsome.

When I came to America, the first guy I thought was cute was mean to me. Probably because I was a late bloomer, but in my mind, I was grown up, so this felt painful. But I'm sure every girl goes through these pains and aches during their teen years, and I was no different. It helped having a best friend to confide in. I had always had one friend who I considered to be my best friend; that person changed through the different seasons of my life depending on my circumstances, but nonetheless, I always had someone who could listen. This was a blessing because I was not comfortable talking to my parents about issues of the heart.

One of those friends was very dear to me as we spent the majority of our early teens together. She was talkative like me and also played in orchestra with me, and we wrote letters to each other, folding them into heart shapes, and exchanging them in church. We looked forward to seeing each other and going places together, as youth would often go somewhere after church. Some days it was Rollerblading, others ice skating, others just walking around downtown. At that time, friends and trips trumped anything else that was going on in my life.

One winter, I went to a sleepover at her house, and we were snowed in. We spent almost a week together because nobody could drive me back home. I had been going through a tough time personally, and I told her about the tall, dark, and handsome guy I had been dating who broke my heart. I was devastated because I thought he would be the guy I'd marry, though I was only fifteen. I was head over heels for him and even gave him my first kiss because I was afraid he would leave me—He said if I didn't kiss him, I didn't love him; so, to prove my love, I did it. I hated myself for giving in, but I didn't want him to leave me. He left me anyway.

This was the first time I compromised the personal standard I had set for myself. There were things I never wanted to do, like drink, smoke, do drugs, and kiss or sleep with anyone before marriage. I still had not smoked, hadn't drank alcohol, hadn't slept with anyone, hadn't done drugs, but I had kissed someone, thinking it would save my relationship, yet I was still rejected.

I didn't know how to cope with the overwhelming emotions, so I began writing poetry. I wrote every day, all the things I remembered from our short-lived dating life, all the emotions I felt, all the desires I had, I put in writing. I listened to non-Christian music about love, which only brought more pain and depression; however, at that time, it seemed like it was helping me cope. I also started dieting, skipping meals, and starving myself in my effort to lose the unwanted weight, which I thought had maybe contributed to my rejection. This was when I started struggling with my eating disorder.

I had not told my friend about the eating disorder at the time because I thought I was in control. I only told her about my heartbreak. She sympathized with my pain and encouraged me to have faith that God had a better plan for me. Her faith was much stronger than mine, and she did not worry about her future husband; instead, she seemed to trust God with that part of her life. I, on the other hand, tried to take matters into my own hands, which only brought rejection and pain.

After the breakup, I started reading the Bible more often in my effort to grow spiritually. I began thinking about baptism. Some of my friends were getting baptized the upcoming summer and I felt like it was my time too. I had a good grasp of the Bible, and though I've never read it completely, I'd practically memorized the gospels and Genesis in my many attempts to start from the beginning. Besides, if I were ever to get married, I would not be allowed unless I was baptized. And who knew, maybe the reason why I couldn't stop sinning completely had to do with baptism. I thought maybe something miraculous happened when I went under water with the Holy Spirit enabling me to never sin again.

I started attending baptism classes and memorizing Bible verses. I understood that baptism was a promise that I was giving to serve God with a good conscious.[29] I thought that by making this promise publicly, I would have to really keep it and maybe it'd give me more motivation to not sin when tempted.

As I started preparing for baptism and getting my life back on track, I met another guy—tall and handsome. To be honest, I'm not sure exactly what attracted me to him at the beginning, maybe just the fact that he noticed me. It felt good to be noticed, especially because I was somewhat still depressed over the last breakup, feeling lonely and brokenhearted.

It happened when my brother and I were on our way to Oregon for another youth conference and we stopped at a rest area. My brother must have already known him because this stranger to me walked up to our car as if he already knew us. We barely spoke though, just exchanged looks of "nice to meet you" and got back on the freeway in our respective cars.

When we arrived, I met his sister. We became good friends with the two of them, with many trips following. With every trip, we got to know each other better, and I grew fond of this tall and handsome guy. He was really careful about making sure people did not know we were together because dating was not allowed in our church unless you were engaged. And we were far from it; only at the point of building a friendship.

I got baptized along with a few of my friends the summer of 1997. It was an interesting experience because right before the baptism, I had to stand up in front of the church for a test to see if I was ready for baptism. I don't remember what exactly was asked of me, but I do remember how someone made comments about my hair being too short. It was confusing to me why the focus was so external, pointed toward how I looked, how many times I had read the Bible, how involved I was in church, how many verses I memorized. Everything was based on my actions and not my personal relationship with the Lord. But no one asked me about how I came to Christ, because if they had, they would have learned that I was trying to save myself by my own works. Nonetheless, at that time, I was glad I made this step. It was an important part of acceptance into the church. The first step was repentance, which needed to happen publicly; the second step was baptism. With each step, the expectation was to live a life honoring God, which I interpreted as living without sin.

Is it really possible to live like that?

I figured it was, since it was not talked about. The only time people talked about someone's specific sin was when they were ex-communicating someone, usually for sex before marriage, affairs, or drug or alcohol addiction. I swore I would never do those things because I would rather die than be shamed in front of the church and be kicked out, never to be allowed to lead any ministry in church. There were reasons for that of course, Bible taught us that leaders must be pure.[30] I have seen people who were ex-communicated and they either left the church completely in shame and shock, went to a different church, or just sat on the back pew for the rest of their life, as if they had an invisible label on them. I made sure I never committed *those* sins because I didn't want to be labeled for the rest of my life.

I was actually ready to have a fresh start in life, yet again. I was now a young woman, just baptized, and I was starting college and a new job. Things were looking up for me. It felt like God was finally happy with my life and beginning to bless me more. I felt like when I was good, God gave me good things, and when I was bad, God gave me bad things and punished me. Since I'd been baptized, was faithfully studying the Bible, teaching Sunday school, and attending to other church commitments, while keeping my bad habits under control, I assumed He was pleased.

I thought that if I did all the right things, it would show that I was seeking God and trying to please Him. And once I pleased Him, He would bless me. And it seemed to be happening. Even my relationship with this tall and handsome guy was progressing; eventually he told me how he felt about me, and we went on a real date. My parents even let me go—I didn't have to sneak out and pretend I was going with my friends, as I had done with the previous guy. Maybe because they respected him and saw him as someone who would honor their daughter. I felt the same way.

Since he lived far from my house, we did not see each other often, but occasionally went on a date within the year and a half of our friendship. Though some lines were crossed, he attempted to draw boundaries, and I respected him for that. After all, I did not want to be ex-communicated. I was excited about his calls and looked forward to seeing him in church. We had this idea, or maybe it was just my dream, to go to the Space Needle on my eighteenth birthday.

A few weeks before my birthday, I started getting worried about our upcoming date. I really looked forward to it and hoped he did too, but I had not seen him in church nor heard from him in weeks. I had never called him myself because it was inappropriate for the girl to initiate; so I waited and waited—nothing. Finally, I decided to get over my pride and give him a call, only to find out that the date was canceled. I did not understand why, but knew this was a breakup, though nothing definitive was said. I was devastated and felt like God had not kept His promise when He said He had good plans for me. I was trying to be good, doing all the right things, though deep down I knew I wasn't good enough. *But why? What have I done wrong?*

As I sobbed that night, my dad came in and turned on a song by Louis Armstrong called "What a Wonderful World." Its words and melody still remind me of the pain I was feeling then.

I see trees of green, red roses too
I see them bloom, for me and you
And I think to myself
What a wonderful world
The colors of the rainbow, so pretty in the sky
Are also on the faces of people going by
I see friends shaking hands, saying how do you do
They're really saying, I love you

The longer I listened, the more I cried, feeling sorry for myself. *How is this a wonderful world, when all I feel is pain and rejection? How is this a wonderful world, when I have to try so hard? How can this be a wonderful world, when I keep messing up my life and can't seem to get it together?* The words *I love you* spoke loudest. And my sweet dad, though he didn't say those words in person, said it through a song. I wanted to be loved, but I failed to realize that Jesus was the only one who could fill that need.

But instead of turning to Him, I turned to my own coping strategies, trying to supress my inadequacy. The troubles I'd had previously with my eating disorder came spiraling back with greater intensity. I couldn't even read the Bible because I felt as if God had abandoned me and was punishing me for my sins. I buried myself in school and work, trying to control the little I had. Early morning, I left for college, went to work right after, and worked till late night. I put on a really strong, solid mask and isolated myself emotionally from the outside world.

I went to another church in pursuit of a different life and different friends so I could forget and move on. It was the church I had gone to with my family originally when we first arrived in the United States, so I knew some people there and they welcomed me. They had a neat youth, with many friendly faces and various opportunities for trips. I particularly loved the trips as they helped me escape my pain.

It wasn't long before one guy from the youth started showing interest in me. He was a smooth talker and was able to talk anyone into pretty much anything. Before I realized what was happening, I was in his car going on a trip with youth because he had convinced me that I should ride with him and leave my car to save gas.

I had no interest in him whatsoever because he was neither tall, dark, nor handsome to me, so I easily agreed. I was also excited about meeting new people and getting to know the church youth since more people had immigrated since I had left. I also felt good about being noticed, and the fact that someone would care about my gas mileage flattered me.

We went on more trips with youth, going to different places almost every Sunday after church, and this guy always managed to get me in his car even though I really didn't want to and sometimes I would intentionally go with someone else just so he would leave me alone. Or I would take my own car and pack it full of other people to make sure I'd be on my own.

I don't remember exactly what trip it was, but I was riding with him again when he told me that God had revealed to him that he was supposed to marry me. I was appalled at his directness, so I decided to be direct with him. I said I wanted nothing to do with him and that it would never work out because I was in love with someone else. He insisted on the fact that I would fall in love with him eventually. We argued back and forth, and I told him exactly how I felt about him—not interested. He didn't seem to mind my aggressive nature, nor my mean comments toward him. It was almost like he liked it, or maybe that was a protective response because he laughed and still insisted we would be married one day.

To be honest, I found it interesting that someone would tolerate so much cruelty and mockery and still not back off. Instead, he started coming over to my work and offering me lunch. I don't even know how he learned about where I worked, but he began calling there and came over almost every day. My boss started to get annoyed by him, and I tried to push him away and tell him to go away, but since he would not take *no* for an answer, I'd give in and tell myself that I could at least get a free lunch out of it.

Those free lunches turned into other types of gifts and eventually I just accepted what he had to offer because he was not backing off. After all, I was hurt enough, why not let him make up for the pain?

At that point, he started following me everywhere. As soon as I left my house, his car would be right there, with him standing in the middle of the street blocking my way. Our conversations usually went something like this:

ME: What do you want?

HIM: Let's go to the mall!

ME: I don't want to go to the mall.

HIM: Let's go for a walk!

ME: I'm busy. I have to go.

HIM: Come, on! Just for a little bit, I want to show you something.

ME: NO!

HIM: YES!

ME: NO!

I would drive away and he would follow. The conversation would start again on the next stop. Eventually I would give in, go for a ride with him, and then tell him never to come back again. Instead, he started calling my home, and then my family began to get annoyed. I'd pick up the phone and the same conversation would take place. He just wouldn't leave me alone. I would drive to college and all of a sudden see a car following me. It was him again. It seemed like he was everywhere.

But, after a while, I somehow got used to it. He knew where I worked, knew where I went to college, and even the times I left and returned. He was "stalking" me to the max, which was disturbing, and I probably should have reached out for help, but something in me was saying, *you can control this situation yourself.*

I had been driving around with him for some time now, but whenever people asked if he was my boyfriend, I would give them a definitive *no.* I was clear and told people he was a friend and not even really that.

One day during our regular family park day, he again found me, and he pulled out a ring and asked me to marry him. It was unexpected but I was not surprised since he kept insisting on the fact that I'd fall in love with him. I declined the proposal and in a strange way it felt good to be on the other side of a rejection.

My public rejection stopped him for a little while. In the meantime, I tried to find other friends, even pretended to date another guy, thinking that would push him away. It worked for a little while, but eventually he came back and continued following me. I was repulsed by him, but I still accepted his advances and bribes because it was easier than constantly arguing back and forth.

As a naive young woman, I did not see the signs of danger. I was trying to fill my need for love, and even though he was not the guy of my dreams, I was selfishly taking advantage of the situation. Instead of trusting God with my future, I turned to my own destructive strategies that stemmed from my shame of being rejected.

What I didn't know then was that God's *good plan* for my life wasn't to meet a guy, get married, and live happily ever after (though that would have been amazing). His good plan was to bring me toward Himself and make me more like Him. How do I know that? It is written in Romans 8:28-29, "And we know that in all things God works for the good of those who love him, who have been called according to his purpose. For those God foreknew he also predestined to be conformed to the image of his Son." There! You see, God was working everything for my own good, to make me conform to the image of His Son, meaning He wanted me to go through trials so I would turn to Jesus and stop relying on my own efforts to find happiness.

And when are we more likely to turn to God? In our happy moments? No. Usually it is the trials that bring us closer to God. Except, at the time, I failed to see that and turned to my own rebellious ways instead.

Jesus understands our pain. He experienced it beyond what any human ever experienced. He understands how it feels to be rejected by people you love. His own family thought He was out of his mind.[31] Jesus also knows what it feels like to suffer in moments of weakness. Hebrews 4:15 says, "For we do not have a high priest who is unable to empathize with our weaknesses, but we have one who has been tempted in every way, just as we are—yet he did not sin." Jesus knows our weaknesses and our temptations because He experienced them Himself.

I still didn't understand this in those trying moments of my life. Instead of turning to Him, I turned to isolation, food, and relationships. I failed to understand that only Jesus could completely fill my deepest need for love. Moreover, He is the only one who loves me unconditionally knowing all my deepest secrets and struggles. In all my relationships, whether with girls or guys, I had never been able to share my deepest secrets because I was afraid of rejection. But Jesus knew those secrets and loved me anyway.

When I got baptized, I thought I was doing it for the right reasons, but in retrospect, the reasons were selfish. Instead of offering myself as a faithful servant to the Lord, I wanted God to serve me. I chased after a relationship, but not with Jesus. I waited for a call, but not from Jesus. I wanted a date, but not with Jesus. I wanted to be loved, by not by Jesus. I wanted the earthly pleasures, the tangible blessings, that I could touch, see, and feel. Jesus seemed so distant and so abstract. I had a head knowledge of Him, but I did not know Him in my heart. I was worshiping God with my lips, but my heart was far from Him. As it says in Matthew 15:8, "These people honor me with their lips, but their hearts are far from me." I never experienced that transformational power within me, not when I repented and not when I got baptized—maybe just for a moment for the remainder of the day, but nothing that lasted more than that. I still sinned and nothing changed because I was putting my faith in my own work. I had done more work to try to outdo my sinning with good and asked forgiveness daily, but I didn't feel anything change. I just felt more exhaustion with every passing year.

I relied on my own works and righteousness for my salvation. I never smoked, never even held a cigarette in my hand, and I was proud. I never drank alcohol—just tried one time, but then repented. At one point I could have said that I had never kissed anyone, but I had messed that up, though I had repented and wouldn't do it again. I had never slept with anyone. I never went to a bar or did drugs. I still had quite a few *nevers* I could use to defend myself. But according to Isaiah 64:6-7, all these righteous acts are filth in God's eyes. They are me trying to say that I'm righteous, all while looking down on people who are struggling with some of these things. When my friends were *trying out* cigarettes and alcohol, I judged them in my heart, thinking that I was somehow better because I didn't try. When my friends were ditching school and I wasn't, I grew proud of being such a good girl. When people offered me alcohol and I told them I didn't drink because I was a Christian, I grew proud. Yet, when I was alone, I knew I was broken and continued to struggle with my addictions.

The real problem was not even the addiction or bad habits. These were only symptoms of a bigger problem. People turn to alcohol or drugs because they are trying to fill a void. People turn to pornography or masturbation because they are trying to numb themselves from another pain that's deep inside their hearts. People turn to food because they are trying to fill a hole in their hearts. That hole could only be filled by Jesus Christ Himself. The real question is this:

What do you turn to in trying to fill the void in your heart?

- Is it relationships?

- Is it food? Alcohol? Drugs?

- Is it sex (whether it comes through internet, spouse, or other places)?

- Is it shopping? Working? Social media? Music?

- Is it anger? Complaining? Gossip? Judgment?

- Is it isolation? Self-harm? Pills?

If you were to evaluate your tendencies when you are experiencing strong emotions, what do you typically do? It may be more than one. What is important is that these are only symptoms that reveal something that needs healing in your life. There might be deep roots of shame that have never been dealt with and the enemy keeps playing the same script in your head, which subconsciously does its damaging work in your life. If you keep ignoring the signs, you will continue to live in the desert, feeling dry, powerless, and worn out. But God wants you to trust Him because He has good plans for you.

The people of Israel, as they wondered in the desert for forty years, turned to their own coping strategies and failed to trust

God, who took them out of slavery in Egypt and demonstrated great miracles along the way. Instead of quickly reaching the promised land, they wandered aimlessly for forty years. All because they lacked faith that God loved them and had good plans for them. I had done exactly the same thing, wandering in my desert all of my teen years and failing to trust God, pursuing my own happiness, and, as a result, feeling empty and hopeless. So whatever trial you might be going through, remember there is a God who has a good plan for you, and that plan is to make you more like Jesus. Only He can fill your deepest need and deliver you from the pain and shame that causes you to turn to your own coping strategies. True happiness is found only in Jesus.

Lie #5:	Things of this world can fill my need for love.
Truth #5:	**Jesus is the only one who can fill my need for love.**

Before you move into the next chapter, reflect on the following questions:

1. What things of this world have you turned to in the past to fill a void in your heart?

2. What things do you still turn to in order to fill a void?

3. What might be the deeper issue that you have not addressed that causes you to turn to these things?

4. Pray the words of Psalm 139:23-24, "Search me, God, and know my heart; test me and know my anxious thoughts. See if there is any offensive way in me and lead me in the way everlasting." Listen to God as He reveals to you the unresolved issues you might need to confess and bring to light.

Chapter 6

Dead End

> *"When I kept silent, my bones wasted away through my groaning all day long."*
>
> **— Psalm 32:3**

When I was six years old, my dad took me and my two older siblings to Moldova, which was two days and two nights away by train from our home in St. Petersburg. Moldova is a warm little country that was part of the Soviet Union at the time and was where much of the country's produce came from. My parents had relatives who lived there, so we visited often during the summer season. While we were there, we stayed near a river where all the kids would swim, and my dad watched us but not carefully since there were many people swimming. I did not know how to swim, so I played on the shore.

On one such visit, I was wearing flip-flops and walking along the shallow part of the river when my flip-flops started to slide off my feet. I tried to keep them on and kept going deeper into the water in my effort to preserve my flip-flops on my feet. Suddenly I was on the bottom of the river looking up with a foot of water above my head, powerless to pull myself up to the top. I wanted to scream but could not open my mouth. I was helpless, running out of breath with water starting to suffocate me, and I knew it would be a matter of minutes before it was over. I saw the light and the surface of the water with people swimming around, but I was completely powerless to pull myself up, and my flip-flops were long gone. This is exactly how I would describe the next segment of my life.

As I was playing around on the shore, I did not realize the river had a tide and it pulled me in. When this man continued to forcefully pursue me—with my resistance making him more insisting—I resolved to accept his advances, telling myself it was on friendly terms, not realizing the potential danger.

What I am about to describe is difficult to remember exactly because I have been actively trying to erase this segment of my life. But there are moments that have remained with me, though they no longer torment me because Jesus have done a great amount of healing in my heart.

I believe it was the Fourth of July and we were watching fireworks in downtown Seattle. It was just the two of us and, as usual, we spent much of that time talking and arguing. As we sat there, he reached out and touched my face. In my mind I felt like I needed to be repulsed by that, but I let it happen.

From that moment on, I felt an invisible bond between us, but I fought back the thoughts because I honestly hated him, and I was not sure why I'd even allowed him to touch me. I wanted nothing to do with him.

On another occasion, he kissed me. I didn't want it, but I again let it happen. That kiss led me to hate him even more, and to loathe myself for allowing it. After it happened, I asked him to take me home and never come see me again.

Despite my request, his visits continued. I can't remember what day it was, but it was after the kiss, and we were driving up to the mountains alone. Usually we went with a group from our youth, but this time it was just him and me. The car was parked and as usual, we talked and argued, and then the unthinkable happened. It happened as fast as me emerging underwater in my effort to save my flip-flops. He was stronger and I went under as the tide pulled me deeper and deeper. Escape was futile because the doors were locked. Where would I have gone even if I did break free? His aggression and determination swept me to the bottom of the river, drowning all my dreams and losing the only flip-flops I had—in that case, my virginity.

After that devastating experience, I want to say the visits were over and I never saw him again. But I would be lying. I came home that night numb, as if I was still underwater. And to tell you the truth, I was, in a metaphorical sense. I was under water for a long time after that. I didn't quite understand what had happened and how it could possibly have happened to me. I was the girl who took pride in having so many *nevers. How could I ever get myself into this mess? How could I ever allow me, a girl who evangelized on the streets and taught Sunday school, to fall this low? How could I?*

I hated myself and the more I hated myself, the more numb I became. In my drowning incident at six years old, someone eventually helped me out and my flip-flops were recovered. But this was not going to be the case now; at least, I didn't see how anything could ever be recovered, and there was no one who could help me in my mess.

If I had told someone, I would have been ex-communicated from the church, just as my sister was before she married her husband. My sister couldn't live with the guilt, so she went to talk to a pastor and confessed her sin. She was told that her secret was safe, but my parents were immediately notified and all hell broke loose. I still remember my sister's panicked voice as she screamed on the phone, calling her boyfriend, "My dad's going to kill you, run!" I get that my dad was angry, I would be furious too, but what wasn't taken into account was that my sister came in confession to be free from her guilt and shame. She had already admitted her guilt. I had so many questions about this: *Isn't that what Jesus died for? To bring freedom to the captives and heal the brokenhearted? Then why do we do the opposite when responding to people's confession of sin? We put stronger chains on them and break their heart a thousand more times, so that they could feel the agony of their sin. Then why did Jesus have to die, if we inflict the same punishment on people who come to Him to be free of sin?*

I understood the Bible taught us about how to treat someone who calls themselves a Christian but is immoral, in 1 Corinthians 5:9-11, "I wrote to you in my letter not to associate with sexually immoral people—not at all meaning the people of this world who are immoral, or the greedy and swindlers, or idolaters. In that case you would have to leave this world. But now I am writing to you that you must not associate with anyone who claims to be a brother or sister but is sexually immoral or greedy, an idolater or slanderer, a drunkard, or swindler. Do not even eat with such people." This means that someone who claims to be a Christian but actively lives an immoral life and promotes that to others needs church discipline and ex-communication. This is someone who hides their sin under the pretense of God's forgiveness. But if a person had stumbled and actually confessed, this is the way of the Christian life. Without that, how could anyone ever be free of sin and shame?

When the Pharisees brought a woman caught in adultery saying that she must be stoned according to the law, Jesus said, in John 8:7, "Let any one of you who is without sin be the first to throw a stone at her." And you know what happened? The oldest started leaving first, and then the younger ones because no one was without sin. When someone comes in confession, there is one thing that person needs—grace—not shame. You know why? Because shame will lead them to continue in their cycle of sin, but grace has the power to break that cycle. And that is exactly why Jesus died such a brutal death and nailed our sin and shame to the cross, giving us a new life in Him.

This unfortunately happens to so many of our young people, and we wonder why they are living such destructive lifestyles, addicted to drugs, sex, and alcohol. It is because we have scared the living headlights out of the them with our church discipline that sends them the message that they are worthless, adding to the shame they already carry. But confession of sin allows healing to happen, but only when we give grace to the person who confesses, just as God already had. It says in James 5:16, "Therefore confess your sins to each other and pray for each other so that you may be healed." Confession blocks the devil from continuing to work in your mind, reminding you about your past mistake, your failure, and your worthlessness, which are all lies. When you conceal sin, you give the enemy room to feed you these lies. It destroys you, as David described in Psalms 32:3, "When I kept silent, my bones wasted away through my groaning all day long."

These thoughts and the fear of being found out and forever denied any part of church life tormented me. I swore that I was going to go to my grave before anyone learned about this. I had never experienced depression to that extent before. I was throwing up food sometimes five times a day. I thought I was going to die from that, and in some ways, I hoped I would. My bones were wasting away, and I groaned all day long. But no one ever knew about my pain. I was a secret sufferer. And what was worse, I continued the destructive cycle of living in sin.

All my dreams of happily ever after vanished. I now faced two options: one, risk being found out and try to move on from this; or two, just marry this person and pretend it never happened. I was so afraid of anyone finding out, I decided that I was going to agree to marry him.

He continued coming after me as I tried to find something that would make me at least like him as a boyfriend. I was still not comfortable with calling him my boyfriend—I didn't like the way he looked—I tried to change his hair style, the outfits he wore, and make him more attractive. *Maybe I can grow to love him, as he has always told me. Maybe he isn't that bad after all.*

My nineteenth birthday was approaching. A lot had happened in one year. I heard rumors that my best friend was now dating the tall and handsome guy. We did grow apart and no longer talked like we used to. Looking back, I see how she was better for him anyway. I just wish I had never even crossed paths with him because he was hers all along. I got lost in my search for love, carried away by emotions.

Since my Space Needle dream with him had fallen through the year before, I was hoping to make up for the loss, and I told the pursuer about it many times. He promised to take me there on my birthday.

That evening, he parked his car near the Space Needle, and we walked. As we approached our destination, I thought about how pathetic I was, trying to force myself to be happy. I was miserable but pretended everything was great. We took the elevator to the restaurant and were seated at a window table. Everything looked amazing but my soul was aching. I ordered what I would have ordered if this was my dream date come true. I tried to display the emotions that I would have had if I was with someone I actually deeply cared about. But everything was fruitless, and I could not fake what wasn't there.

As we finished dinner, we went up to the observation deck. This is where he proposed again. I guess I somewhat expected it because I was less defiant and rude, but I was not prepared to give an answer. I mean, I already had an answer, and it was a definite *no* in my heart, but in my mind, I was calculating the cost of both options.

If I agreed to marry him, I reasoned that I would be doing what I thought God wanted me to do, since I had already become *one flesh* with this man. By being obedient to God, I would get blessed and have kids. My punishment would be marrying someone I didn't love and maybe that would be enough to appease God and the people in church, if they did find out about my sin someday.

If I said *no*, I would risk being found out, shamed, and forever banished from church, maybe not completely, but I would never be able to serve or lead anything. This was the policy in our church at that time, or at least that was what I thought. Anyone in leadership had to have a good life record since they were supposed to be role models. And with my record, the only position available would probably be—Well, I'm not sure if there would have been any actually. The only positive thing about choosing to decline the proposal was a slight hope that maybe there was a chance I would marry someone I would actually love. That sounded so much better than the first option, but I did not want to ruin the date I had tried so hard to re-create, so I said *yes*, hoping that I could take it back after the day was over.

As we descended from the observation deck and walked toward his car, I begged God to give me a sign about whether what I was doing was right. When we reached our parking spot, his car was gone—it had gotten towed away and we spent another few hours trying to get it back—and I took that as a sign that I was making a big mistake. So, while all this was happening, I was planning my escape. *How am I going to take my answer back? My parents will probably flip out if they learn I agreed to marry him.* I mean, they knew about me spending a lot of time with him, but they had no idea what had happened between us. They also knew that I hated him and never wanted anything to do with him, *so how was I supposed to tell them that I was now going to marry him?* Then I thought that maybe if I did tell them, and they were okay with it, that would be a sign from God that this was the right thing to do.

So, once we made it home, I worked up some courage and told my mom about the proposal and that I was thinking about marrying him. I told her that I was wrong about him and that he was not that bad, that I actually liked him. It was a lie, but I was really trying to convince myself, and maybe with more convincing, I would finally believe it.

When my mom heard what I said, she became furious. She could not believe I had made such a rash decision without thinking it through. She told me, "Don't you know that you have to sleep with this guy for the rest of your life?" Sadly, I knew and wasn't thrilled about that either.

My mom's reaction gave me more motivation to give the ring back and tell him it was never going to work out. However, the news of our engagement had already spread somehow. I remember walking around the college campus and running into my best friend who was now dating my ex; she congratulated me on my engagement. I wanted to scream that it was all a lie and I hated the guy. With my eyes filling up with tears, I just smiled and pretended to be happy. *How did it go this far? How do people know?* I was confused and disheartened because it felt like a done deal. *What if it is? What if I just let it all happen and numb myself in the process?* I was good at faking now. My mask grew thicker with every passing day. I lived one life on the outside and a different life on the inside, and I didn't see how this marriage would be any different. I could never expose my deepest pain, my failure, my guilt and shame.

I kept going with the flow and just pretending everything was fine, but inside I was dying. I just wanted to end it all. I wanted a way out. *Maybe the only way out is to take my own life?* I was already hurting my health with my eating disorder and I didn't even try to stop because I wanted it to kill me. I wanted to get hit by a truck and just end it in an instant. I didn't want it to be my own suicide, I just wanted something to kill me because I was afraid of going from one hell to another if I committed suicide. I was taught that all suicides are destined for hell, and I didn't want that option.

I remember feeling really sick because of the eating disorder. I just didn't feel good. I thought maybe I would finally die, which was a relief, but I was also guilt stricken by that thought and couldn't stop thinking about what I was doing to my family. I decided the least I could do was write my mom a goodbye letter. I was not ready to tell my dad because I was always scared by his anger and knew he would be better off not knowing what was going on with me. So I just wrote to Mom. I told her how sorry I was for being such a screw-up. That I was sorry I was even born. That maybe I was meant to drown. I told her I wasn't making the right choices and the damage I had caused could never be repaired, and I did not know how to get out of this situation.

I sobbed as I inked this letter. I wanted to tell her how much I loved her and how much I cherished everything she had ever done for me. She had always taken such good care of us. There was not a day when she didn't have a warm meal for us or something yummy for us to enjoy. She made sure we had a variety of stylish clothes and shoes. She didn't just buy us what we needed, but always spoiled us with what we wanted. *How can I let her down?* I wondered. I knew she would be so disappointed with me if she knew what I had done. But what's done is done and I had hit a dead end.

I prayed asking God for mercy yet again. I didn't want to live like this. I didn't want a marriage without love, and I didn't want to live a lie. I wanted to be loved, with all my failures. I was tired of living a double life. I wanted another chance. I had really gone deep down the valley of sin and I couldn't rescue myself, just like I could not rescue myself on the bottom of that river. The only thing I could do was stare up and see the light, hoping someone would see me and rescue me. I begged for forgiveness again, surrendered all I had left to God, and honestly hoped he would just take me home that night.

Looking back now, over twenty years later, I still tear up as I, in a sense, re-live those moments. Moments where I felt all hope was gone and there was nothing left to live for. I never planned for that, nor did I ever imagine that something like that could happen to me. All I wanted was to be loved, by God and by people, and I had done everything to deserve the opposite. I was sure God was disappointed with me and if anyone ever found out about me, I was sure they would shake their heads in disgust.

Hopelessness was my new reality as I continued living my double life. If you had known me at that time, you would have probably never guessed that I was going through the most difficult time of my life. I continued attending church and pretending everything was okay. I continued wearing my mask—and it was itching my face because inside I was in hell.

Have you ever felt hopeless? I'm sure you have had moments when life pulled you in a direction you didn't plan to go. When all of a sudden you were in over your head and had to figure out how to pull yourself out. But what if you didn't know how or have the strength for it? That is true hopelessness. It is when you realize that your options are limited and the options you do have will only drown you further.

Let me explain what I mean by that. I could have gone to my parents or even the pastors and told them all of what was happening to me. I could have confessed all my guilt and shame. Yes, that is absolutely true. However, not much would have changed because the problem was with me. I was believing a lie about God and about myself. I thought I sinned too much and that I no longer qualified for His grace. In fact, I sinned after my baptism. The way I saw it at the time was that if this had happened before my baptism and then I'd repented publicly and gotten baptized, I would have been all good and accepted into the church. But I had broken my pledge and sinned after my baptism, which caused me to feel unsurpassable guilt and shame. This was the lie I was believing that perpetuated the cycle of sin in my life and left me with a spirit of hopelessness.

What I didn't know was that when Jesus died on the cross two thousand years ago, He died for all my sins, not just the sins that I committed before I repented, or the sins of my past. He died for my sins that I am committing in the present, and the sins I will commit in the future. He paid for all my sins!

This is why right before Jesus died, He said, "It is finished!" as recorded by John 19:30. According to the commentary in the

121

Holman Christian Standard Bible, this phrase has a significant impact because it is not only the past sins that are forgiven, but the present and the future. It states, "The verb is in the perfect tense, signifying something accomplished in the past with continuing results in the present and future."[32] It is not partially finished or partially paid, as I understood, but fully. Psalm 103:12 even puts it this way, "As far as the east is from the west, so far has he removed our transgressions from us." If west and east could ever come together, then our sins and ourselves would also be able to come together and accuse us. Just like east and west are polar opposites and could never cross, our sins are also not able to cross the path with our salvation, because Jesus took care of them all on the cross. Romans 8:1-2 support this notion, "Therefore, there is now no condemnation for those who are in Christ Jesus, because through Christ Jesus the law of the Spirit who gives life has set you free from the law of sin and death." What is beautiful about this verse is that there is no time stamp on this. The *now* it refers to does not depend on your behavior. *Now* means that if you are in Christ, you never stand condemned, regardless of what sins you committed or will still commit. This is something that I did not understand. I thought Jesus only died for my past sins, but that all the future sins could still push me into hell.

This is why so many people around us continue living in the destructive patterns of sin. Let's take my brother as an example. He has accepted Jesus into his life but continues to struggle with drug addiction. He is perceived as someone who loses his salvation and therefore needs to repent by quitting his drug addiction and receiving his salvation again.

The problem with this mentality is that my brother will never be able to stop his drug addiction until he stops believing the lie that he lost his salvation in the first place. This lie is what keeps him in his cycle of addiction. The root cause of his behavior is shame, which he keeps suppressed by turning to drugs. The shame he feels is legitimate and is a natural emotion when he fails to reach a certain standard, which in his case, is failing to live up to his resolve of never turning to drugs. The moment he fails, he goes on a downward spiral because once he misses his perfect streak, the voice immediately confirms what he already believes about himself: that he is worthless, useless, and inadequate, and therefore was never a child of God. By believing this lie, he acts in line with his thinking. Remy Diederich (2006), in his book *Healing the Hurts of Your Past*, explains how the only way to have freedom from the curse of sin and shame is by not believing the lies of the enemy.[33] It has to do with understanding your true identity in Christ, that you are a child of God with a God-given purpose for your life. It is about being saved by faith, not by your own futile effort in controlling sin.

Let's take my uncle as another example. He has struggled with alcohol addiction all of his life though he grew up in a Christian family. He repented multiple times, yet he continues to struggle with this addiction. The root problem is not his addiction itself; he can't break this addiction because of his faulty thinking that somehow he can reach a level of sobriety that will allow him to earn the calling of being God's child. In reality, if he believed that he was already a child of God, and if people treated him as such, he would be able to live in that new identity, believing that no amount of trying to be sober and no amount of promises and perfect days could make him any more acceptable than he already is, in Christ. His issue is not the addiction, but his belief, and in his case, the family's beliefs about him, which probably further confirm what he already thinks about himself.

Fortunately, there is good news, and you know why it's so good? Because Jesus died for all your sins and you are His child, even on the most sinful day of your life. You never stop being His child, even when you turned to drugs, or alcohol, or anything else for that matter, to numb your pain and shame. Claiming your new identity in Christ as someone who has value, who is capable, and who is worthy, is what gives you the freedom to live for the purpose you were meant to live for.

You have been created by God and He paid the ultimate price for you to be His child. You are not defined by your struggle with sin, your addiction, your abuse, or your brokenness. You have worth that is determined by God Himself because He thought of you even before you were born, "All the days ordained for me were written in your book before one of them came to be" (Psalms 139:16).

It cost God His own Son to pay for you with His priceless blood. The cost for you is priceless, which makes you priceless. You have so much value that it is not even possible to compare with anything in this world. That is how much you are worth. That is how much I was worth, even in the biggest failure of my life. I based my identity on my performance and the opinions of others. My performance hit rock bottom, and I already knew the opinions others had of me, so I felt worthless and I continued to live out that worthlessness in how I coped with my shame.

But you do not have to live like I did, suffering for many more years ahead. You can claim freedom today. This is why I am so passionate about writing this book. I wish that I had known then what I know now, that God was not angry with me, that He did not disown me, that He did not look at me with disappointment and anger while holding a punishing rod. Instead, He was with me in my sadness because I did not know the truth and believed a lie. He was telling me all along that this was why He had to die. The punishment had already been received by God Himself, on the cross. If I had placed my faith in Him rather than in my performance, I would have probably never even ended up on the path I did.

If you find yourself in a hopeless situation today, know you are not alone. You can claim your true identity by accepting the truth that Jesus died for your past, present, and future sins. There is never a dead end in Christ because He has taken the dead end out of your lifespan and given you a gateway into eternity by His death and resurrection. Even if you find yourself to be the person who has caused harm to someone else, who has hurt someone or made them do something they did not want to do for whatever reason, God has a purpose for you. You do not have to keep hiding and shaming yourself for what you have done or are still doing but can receive the grace that is available and be freed from the guilt and shame that bonds you. Not only that, but God can take any mess and use it for His own glory to give hope to those that may be going through the same experience. And if you find yourself in neither one of those situations, but rather in the place of judgment, thinking how someone could fall this low, there is grace for you too. Even if you had never experienced such depths of sin, sin is sin, no matter how terrible. So instead of being in the judgment seat, offer grace because that is what a sinner needs to experience transformation, which is what Jesus had done for you and me.

Use this time to reflect on God's promises because God has a plan for your life and He wants to use your story, even your deepest pain and your greatest sin. He is the only one who can take what is broken and restore it. Isaiah 61:1-3 are my favorite verses in the Bible and are the theme of this book, spoken by Jesus Himself, "The Spirit of the Sovereign Lord is on me, because the Lord has anointed me to proclaim good news to the poor. He has sent me to bind up the brokenhearted, to proclaim freedom for the captives and release from darkness for the prisoners, to proclaim the year of the Lord's favor and the day of vengeance of our God, to comfort all who mourn, and provide for those who grieve in Zion—to bestow on them a crown of beauty instead of ashes, the oil of joy instead of mourning, and a garment of praise instead of a spirit of despair. They will be called oaks of righteousness, a planting of the

Lord for the display of his splendor." What is most amazing about these verses is that He wants to do all these things for you for the purpose of displaying His splendor. You are God's glory and He will use your life, no matter how broken, and how dark, because He came to earth exactly for that reason, to heal your broken heart, to give you freedom, to comfort you, and to place a crown of beauty on you. Jesus specializes in taking your biggest mess and making it into a message.

Lie #6:	Jesus only paid for my past sins. I have to keep a perfect record after coming to Christ.
Truth #6:	**Jesus paid for my past, present, and future sins.**

Before you move into the next chapter, reflect on the following questions:

1. Think about a time you felt hopeless, what were the thoughts that traveled through your head?

2. How does the truth that Jesus not only paid for your past sins, but also your present and future sins, affect your understanding of God?

3. How does this truth affect your view of self?

4. How does this truth affect your view of other people?

Chapter 7

The Pit of Despair

> *"[He] forgives all your sins and heals all your diseases,*
> *who redeems your life from the pit and crowns you*
> *with love and compassion, who satisfies you with good*
> *things so that your youth is renewed like the eagle's."*
>
> **— Psalm 103:3-5**

I woke up the morning after I wrote my mother the letter feeling somewhat disappointed that God hadn't taken me, but at the same time with a little more hope. I resolved to give the ring back and break off the engagement. However, I knew he would not accept it, especially after I had agreed. He was very forceful and insistent when I went against what he thought should happen, so I was somewhat afraid to back out.

But after my night of surrender, I felt a wave of strength. I wrapped the ring in a bigger box to make it look like a present. I said I had a gift for him and just needed to drop it off quickly because I was in a hurry.

What I anticipated would happen, did, and he did not let me go until he opened the gift, giving it right back to me, saying I needed to rethink it. He said if I didn't take it back, he would throw it in the trash and on and on with his convincing arguments about why I should marry him. I was sick of it. I was done. I wanted out and there was no talking me into marrying him.

Despite his antics, I left, and I don't remember exactly what happened after, but I think he started dating someone else. I started attending an American church because I wanted to avoid any opportunity of running into him, though he knew where to find me. I started seeing another guy, mainly because I wanted to make it clear to the pursuer that it was over for good. I thought maybe this could be my happily ever after. Maybe I didn't have to be the perfect girl everyone expected me to be. I could be who I was, with all my failures, and this new man would hopefully accept me. Besides, he didn't grow up in a religious environment like me; I felt more grace in his eyes and thought I could actually get over my past. We went out on a few dates, and though everything seemed to be going okay, I didn't feel right about it. We soon parted ways but remained on good terms.

The pursuer came back for me, just as I expected he would, as if he never left. I was back in his cage again. Everywhere I went, his car tailgated me. It could be six o'clock in the morning as I was driving to my early college class, and he'd be right behind me. Same thing would happen as it always had with a sickening ending. It was a vicious cycle and I was stuck with absolutely no way out.

The only thing that kept me going was school. I was about to graduate with my associate degree and transfer to the University of Washington. The change of scenery excited me, and I focused on that to avoid completely drowning in my despair. This is when my best friend from Russia, Natasha, who now lived in Sacramento, invited me to check out Fresno Pacific University, a college she was attending at the time. We stayed in touch through letters even though we lived in different states.

I had never even considered moving away, but the idea of moving to another state gave me slight hope that I could put my past behind me. I told my parents about it and they did not object, though it was uncommon for a girl in our culture to move away before getting married. However, they probably sensed my depression and also didn't want me marrying the pursuer.

Before I moved to Fresno, Natasha gave me a gentle warning about the culture of Fresno youth being focused on school, rather than marriage. She said, "If you're looking for a guy, this may not be the best place because all the guys are nice here, but they are not looking to get married. They will give you flowers, take you out, and help you with whatever you need, but it doesn't mean anything." In Fresno, the pressure was not toward marriage but toward education, which was my focus at the time, so I felt like it was the right place for me. Besides, I was trying to run away from a relationship, not jump into a new one. I appreciated the warning, but at the same time, I couldn't imagine that was completely true.

When my parents drove me to the airport, just as I expected, the pursuer showed up as well, accompanied by his friend. I didn't know he was going to be there, but knowing him, I also felt like he could show up anywhere at any time. At that point, almost two years had passed with me living in this nightmare. Every time I saw a car that looked anything like his, I'd startle, and my heart would race. I was ready to finally put an end to this fear and dysfunction. Little did I know that this fear would continue to haunt me for many more years.

As soon as I moved to Fresno in June of 2000, I began a life of work for God. I thought maybe if I got involved in church and served more, I would feel vindicated for my failures. Maybe if people did find out about my past, they would not judge me as much because they would see how I had changed. I write this in retrospect though, because at that time, I was not aware of what I was doing. It was all done on a subconscious level; I was trying to outdo my wrongs with rights.

That summer, the Slavic church was organizing a kids' camp and I signed up to be a counselor. It was amazing to get back into church life and feel needed and accepted. When the camp was over and the school year began, I got involved in a Slavic club on campus, which was basically organizing activities for Slavic people. I also attended every Bible study and church service at the church. I joined the church orchestra and played violin since I was already playing in the Baroque orchestra at the university. I even organized a Russian school at the church. I was very busy, trying to fill my entire time with activity. The non-stop activity also helped me cope with my inner turmoil.

I was quickly accepted into this new community. The church people loved me because I was leading Russian school. My friends liked me because I was very social and involved. And my friend was right about the guys there. They too liked me— just as a friend, of course—and they were very nice. Whenever I needed a car, since I didn't have one, I could ask any guy, and they would either drive me or let me borrow their car. They were generous and often paid for me and others when we were out eating or attending different functions. The culture in Fresno was very positive among youth.

For my twentieth birthday—my first birthday away from home—all the Slavic people came to the Russian house, which was basically a university-provided house where five Russian guys lived. We called it that because Russian college students would just come and hang out there all the time. These guys, who were also very talented, picked up musical instruments, and played me a happy birthday song. I felt very special that day. Of course, even among these new friends, nobody knew me on a personal level, they only saw my beautiful mask. At times, someone would notice something about me and ask if I was okay, and I would immediately smile and say I was great. After all, I had gotten pretty good at wearing my mask by then.

But what was under the mask had gotten even more frightening. I was severely struggling with an eating disorder and because of the shame that now came with the eating disorder, I started taking pills to help me sleep at night. These were pills my mom gave me when I moved to Fresno, saying to only use them in case of really bad pain. So at first I didn't think anything of them, but I had gotten a headache once and tried taking one—and it did magical things. It not only took away my pain, but I felt like I was floating on clouds, in a euphoric kind of state. I slept so well that night that I took them again. They especially helped me deal with my shame after binging and purging. I started to worry about being addicted to them, so I only took them on really bad days. Besides, I didn't have that many to go around, so I tried to use them sparingly.

Fortunately, the pills and the eating disorder didn't seem to interfere with my day-to-day living. I got a job at a coffee shop as a barista, which turned out to be a place where many of my friends went to study or just hang out. The owners of the coffee shop would allow me to have private parties for youth as long as they paid for drinks. So many people came through that coffee shop and so many memories were built. Life seemed good from an outside perspective. I had friends, a place to live, a job, a church family, and a promising future after college.

The following summer, I had an opportunity to go on a mission trip to Russia with a group from Sacramento. I always wanted to be a missionary, considering my evangelistic background, but with the recent circumstances, I hadn't been able to lift my head out of my prison of guilt and shame. This was my chance to redeem myself and do something for God in a bigger way. I dedicated my entire summer toward this mission. We organized camps for kids in orphanages and shared the good news of the Gospel with them.

By the end of camp, all of the girls I worked with had accepted Jesus into their hearts. However, they did not immediately stop their bad habits of smoking or stealing, though many of them tried. I expected them to do just that, but then realized this was exactly what had happened to me. I too expected to stop all my sins and habits after accepting Jesus, but it was not about stopping the behavior. It was about allowing God to transform your mind and heart so that you no longer had to turn to this behavior for self-medication.

All of our dysfunctional behavior is a symptom of a bigger problem rooted in our hearts, and we try to medicate the problem with cigarettes, alcohol, drugs, food, sex, or even hard work for God. I was still medicating with food (gaining a whole twenty pounds over the course of the mission trip), pills to help me sleep, and my active ministry.

I came back from the mission trip still in my pit of despair. I thought doing something great for God would make me feel better and would somehow help me overcome my struggles.

But no matter how hard I tried, I couldn't do it. I made so many promises and I broke those promises the same day, as soon as I felt my shame surface. Diederich (2006) explains this cause-and-effect relationship between shame and the dysfunctions we experience in day-to-day living. He uses a metaphor of a toolbelt with three types of tools: pain preventers, pain killers, and pain expressions.[34]

Pain preventers help you stay in control and could be things like people-pleasing, all-or-nothing behaviors, and perfectionism. According to Diederich (2006), people-pleasing is "when you get out of your way to make people happy, even at your own expense, just so that you don't have to bear the pain of their rejection."[35] It seems like this should be a good thing because you are doing things for others, but without realizing, this person is trying to prevent their shame from rising to the surface from a possibility of being rejected, so they keep doing things because it ensures that people like them and thus helps them feel valued.

I learned this about myself this past winter, when I went on a cruise with five ladies. One of the ladies from Belarus, Angelika, is a woman's life coach and consultant in psychosomatics. She helps women find their God-given purpose so they can live full and happy lives. She took us through a number of sessions where we learned things about ourselves and the patterns of thought we experience. The girls gave me the nickname "chameleon" because I was so eager to please everyone as I tried to fit in with this completely new group of friends whom I had recently met through a friend from Sacramento. I didn't realize I was people-pleasing until they pointed it out. When they asked what we wanted to do during the day, I'd wait until someone responded and then I'd go along with that response, even if I didn't want to do that. In my mind though, I talked myself into wanting to do what they wanted, so it felt like I did want to do it. When we ordered food and someone offered to share a plate with me, I'd agree on what they wanted, even if I didn't want it, as long as they were happy. Of course, I would tell myself that I actually wanted it and suppress my feelings.

One particular time, toward the end of our cruise, we put on our bathing suits and went to the front of the ship to sunbathe. It was very windy. All the girls decided they just wanted to stay covered up and sit in a cozy corner free of wind. But when Angelika asked if someone wanted to go lay in the sun, I agreed to go; after all, I already had my swimwear on.

We sunbathed for a few minutes and I started getting really cold. I did not want to get sick after the cruise, so I thought maybe I needed to get out of this wind. I asked Angelika if she was cold, hoping she would say *yes* and we would both go back. When she said *no*, I was a little disappointed but did not want to leave her because I didn't want her to think that I didn't care about her, so I covered myself with a towel and kept laying out. I was really uncomfortable, but I was afraid to leave because I would risk someone being upset with me. But as I laid there, freezing, I realized what I was doing, and it confirmed what the ladies were telling me all along. I got up and told Angelika that I was cold and was going back to where it was warm. She just said, "okay" and went back to sunbathing. I left, and tried to let it go, but I still felt uneasy about it.

Later that evening, I shared my experience with the ladies while waiting in line for dinner. Angelika wasn't with us in line and when she came, the ladies asked her about how she felt when I left her all alone sunbathing. She said she'd been totally fine, which confirmed that the problem was completely with me and how I perceived myself. This is people-pleasing. Earlier in this book, I shared my other preventive strategies such as perfectionism, when I wasted perfectly new notebooks because of one mistake, and all-or-nothing behaviors, when if I wasn't first or didn't feel like I was winning a game, I'd just opt out. All of these were ways that I tried to control my shame from surfacing.

But what do we turn to when shame has already surfaced? Diederich (2006) calls these tools painkillers, which look different for different people but have some common strategies, and include avoiding uncomfortable subjects, numbing, medications such as drugs and alcohol, keeping secrets, caretaking, intellectualizing or spiritualizing, and minimizing.[36] I have used a number of these and probably still do. Particularly numbing. I never realized that the reason why I have always kept a crazy busy life was because I was trying to numb the pain of my shame, my emotions that arose when I was home alone. Staying busy helped me numb that pain. I also self-medicated with pills and food, as you learned earlier, which gave me a window of escape, though only temporarily.

The last category, according to Diederich (2006), for dealing with shame, if you can't control it or deny it, is to express it. This is something I have seen not only in myself, but in people around me. These tools include envy, anger, rage, panic or anxiety attacks, accepting abuse, self-pity, eating disorders, and suicide.[37] This was eye-opening for me because I have seen all of these behaviors in both Christians and non-Christians, and many of these have surfaced in my life. But the root of the issue is undealt shame, based in the lies we believe about ourselves. When we feel worthless, we will treat ourselves as such, which also spills out onto others. We have all heard the phrase, "hurt people hurt people." The dysfunction we experience in our lives is a direct result of the unresolved sin and shame in our hearts.

This was my life in my early twenties, stuffing my shame while trying to be a good girl. I would sit in church and listen to these beautiful songs about God's grace and I would cry. I knew about God's grace, but I didn't know how to live in this grace, how to be free from sin and shame, how to not have to cover up my insecurities and inability to live without sin. I'd go to a wedding and look at the happy couple and become so angry with myself for messing up my life. I actually hated weddings because they reminded me of the perfection I could never attain. The wedding dress was white because it represented purity. I'd think, *How can I be married in a white dress? I'm not worthy of that because I am not pure. I'm damaged goods, worthless.*

I did not think I could ever stop with my dysfunction and would forever feel like a failure. No amount of Bible reading was helping me. I'd go on these perfect streaks and then fail and give up. I just couldn't stop making bad choices, and I continued feeling worthless. Having a fresh start, yet again, didn't help me. No amount of work I was doing for God was helping me either. Though on the outside, my mask was solid, on the inside I was a wreck, terrified to let anyone in on my deep secrets. *If they only knew my past, they would probably unfriend me, and I'd be thrown out of the church. Who would love me knowing everything I have done? And what is more frightening, who would love me knowing my sin struggles now?*

I thought my sins were such horrible sins and that nobody else around me struggled with sin, or if they did, it didn't seem to cause any discomfort for them. I remember I was talking to someone and they were sharing how someone they knew left their wife with six children and had an affair with another woman. This person was so shocked and couldn't believe someone who was Christian could possibly do that. I also hear people talk about others who smoke, drink, or do drugs, basically condemning these people as if they are for sure going to hell. What I never hear about is people being shocked when someone yells at their kids in anger or breaks the speed limit or doesn't put a belt on when they drive. Isn't all wrongdoing sin? It is important to understand what sin is because without it, we might be fighting the wrong enemy, concerned with things that only perpetuate the lies we believe.

Sin is sin. There is no big sin, no little sin. All sin, whether small or big, separates us from a holy God. God and sin are incompatible. They can never stand together. I thought sin was just my actions or thoughts that made me feel bad about myself, but it is more than that. Actions are the fruit that stem from a root that is my flawed nature that supresses the truth, as recorded in Romans 1:18, "The wrath of God is being revealed from heaven against all the godlessness and wickedness of people, who suppress the truth by their wickedness." This is all of us. There is not one who does not do that. Romans 3:10 says, "As it is written: There is no one righteous, not even one." I always thought these verses were for *those* people, the unrighteous and godless, but because I grew up in a Christian family, I was never like that. I always knew God, so I did not suppress the truth. Well, according to my life and the struggles I've experienced, no matter how Christian my family was, I still supressed the truth. I believed lies and those lies produced the behavior I didn't want in me.

John Piper, a pastor and theologian, provides a thorough explanation of the root of sin in his sermon called *What is Sin? The Essence and Root of All Sinning*, defining sin as, "The glory of God not honored. The holiness of God not reverenced. The greatness of God not admired. The power of God not praised. The truth of God not sought. The wisdom of God not esteemed. The beauty of God not treasured. The goodness of God not savored. The faithfulness of God not trusted. The promises of God not believed. The commandments of God not obeyed. The justice of God not respected. The wrath of God not feared. The grace of God not cherished. The presence of God not prized. The person of God not loved."[38] He bases this definition on Romans 1:28-31, "Furthermore, just as they did not think it worthwhile to retain the knowledge of God, so God gave them over to a depraved mind, so that they do what ought not to be done. They have become filled with every kind of wickedness, evil, greed and depravity. They are full of envy, murder, strife, deceit and malice. They are gossips, slanderers, God-haters, insolent, arrogant and boastful; they invent ways of doing evil; they disobey their parents; they have no understanding, no fidelity, no love, no mercy." This is a good description of our nature: we are corrupt or have a depraved mind. This is who we are without God. Our shame stems from this identity, so do all of our actions in managing our shame.

In his sermon, Piper goes on to explain that sinning comes from the root of this God-ignoring nature, and defines it as, "Any feeling or thought or speech or action that comes from a heart that does not treasure God over all other things."[39] To treasure God over all other things, one must believe God exists and believe in the work He had done to redeem us from our condition. This again all comes down to faith and our beliefs about God and who we are in Him. If we believe that He has died for us and accept His sacrifice in exchange for our sin, we become a new creation, born again. Our identity is now rooted in God, by grace through faith. It comes back to this verse in Hebrews 11:6 again, "Without faith it is impossible to please God, because anyone who comes to him must believe that he exists and that he rewards whose who earnestly seek him."

When we understand that sin is not just an action, but is our nature that denies God, no matter how religious one might be, then we can understand the magnitude and significance of the cross. If the root of our sin is not the things we do, but the nature we have, then focusing on trying to stop a sin is pointless. You can never stop sinning, unless you put your faith in Christ and start believing in your new identity. The only way that can happen is if we stop focusing on defining other people by their sins and instead focus on who they are in Christ, no matter what their sin is. It will also happen if we stop sweeping sin under the rug; instead, expose sin by sharing the freedom we received through Jesus.

People like to classify sin into categories from "most severe"— i.e., deserving punishment and public shame—to "not so bad"—i.e., no need to even bring it up. Based on these categories, people try to manage their lives by avoiding the big sins and trying to be good and righteous by following certain rules.

The truth is that trying to manage sin and creating rules to avoid it is like rearranging chairs on the titanic. The ship will still sink because the only way to deal with the issue of sin is to address the root or the nature of where the sin is coming from, which can only be done by accepting the gift of salvation and living in the new identity. Romans 6:23 says, "The wages of sin is death, but the gift of God is eternal life through Christ Jesus our Lord." Sin is deeply rooted in our shame, whether it is small or big, and it destroys our lives. That's why the verse states that "the wages of sin is death." Death is the opposite of life. If Jesus came to bring you life, sin will destroy your life and take away your joy.

Have you ever met Christians who don't have any joy? That was me for a very long time. And you know why? Because I was dealing with my sin and shame in my own strength. I was trying to prevent it from surfacing, to kill it if it surfaced, and if I couldn't kill it, I'd let it out by making a mess of myself and others. It typically looks something like this: I keep a busy life to numb my feelings and prevent them from surfacing, I eat to feel better when it does surface, and I lash out in anger when I feel like things are going out of control.

I have encountered many Christian people who talk about sin as if it is something that they want to do, but keep under control by avoiding certain places, certain drinks, and certain people. They put a barrier between themselves and the world that could somehow tempt them to sin. When in reality, sin is not outside of us. It is within us. It is our desires that wage war inside our bodies. It says in James 1:14, "But each person is tempted when they are dragged away by their own evil desire and enticed." On one hand, I get it, because sin has a way of temporarily giving us what we think we need: relief, pleasure, a sense of joy, security. That is absolutely true, it is providing us a way to deal with our pain. But the truth is, it is temporary and destructive. It is a lie we believe. It will destroy our health, relationships, and even livelihood. Anyone who has trusted in sin for their happiness knows the outcome and the disappointment it brings. Any person who has experienced living in sin—and all of us have—but then found relief, pleasure, joy, and security in Christ will never want to trade it for the temporary pleasures of sin, though the flesh might still win out sometimes. Only in Christ, not religion, we can have this freedom.

This was the problem with my understanding of grace and what Jesus did to destroy sin. He took care of my shame, which is the root cause of all my sin and dysfunction, so I no longer have to feel worthless and look for relief in pills, food, anger, people-pleasing, and keeping busy. The only thing I need to do is believe that He did all that, that He canceled all of my debt for all of my dysfunction, and that my identity does not depend on my behavior. Now the verse from John 3:16 makes much more sense, "For God so loved the world that he gave his one and only Son, that whoever believes in him should not perish but have eternal life."

I basically need to stop allowing my actions to define who I am, and instead focus on who I am in Christ—then actions will follow. This was difficult to grasp because all of my life, I was told that I was defined by my actions. If I sinned, I was shamed, thinking I must have not been saved. Doubting my salvation was causing all my sin issues. Now that I understand who I am and that I am saved even when I stumble and sin, I am free from the curse of sin and shame. As a result, I have the power to sin less, though will never stop sinning. The more I live by faith and believe this truth, the more I will be able to overcome the enemy and the temptation to sin.

All it takes is the belief that God had paid for all your sin and shame and that you are a brand-new creation, no longer depraved, nor worthless, incapable of doing anything that would make you unworthy of heaven, even when you fall short (because you will as long as you are in your fleshly body). What this means is that our entire life is now based on our faith in this single truth. This is what it means to live by faith. And when we live by faith, meaning we believe we are God's children, we no longer have to stuff our shame, deny our shame, or express our shame in unhealthy ways, because we are free in Christ. Galatians 5:16 support this notion, "So I say, walk by the Spirit, and you will not gratify the desires of the flesh." Walking by the Spirit means being empowered by His truth daily, and He will give you what you need. It does not mean you will never sin or struggle with shame. The battle against sin will still happen because the enemy will want to instill doubt, but you will have the power from God to overcome these doubts by knowing your true identity. Moreover, you will have the wisdom and power to not wallow in your sin because your sin will not ruin your identity in Christ. The only reason why we wallow in our sin and keep going back is because we begin to think we are not worthy. You are still worthy, forever worthy; it is in those times where it requires the most faith.

If you are still trying to please God by your good behavior, trying your best not to sin, you will eventually wear out because you will never be able to please God with just your own effort and strength. You are living by a religious belief. The only way you can please Him is if you trust in Him by faith. Ephesians 2:8-9 says, "For it is by grace you have been saved, through faith—and this is not from yourselves; it is the gift of God—

not by works, so that no one can boast." The only thing that happens when you try to live by your good intentions of not sinning is that you become proud and self-righteous, like the Pharisees. But when you acknowledge your tendencies toward sin and allow God to transform you, starting with your thought patterns, and then your actions, you truly begin living solely by faith. And this is the life that pleases God.

I am grateful that I did wake up that morning and that God did not take me home yet. He had so much more planned for me in the next twenty years that I can testify to, and I'm sure He has more to come in the future, for however many years He will allow me to live. Being in the pit of despair allowed me to experience the depth of my sin and understand how precious is the blood that ransomed me. I pray that you also recognize how precious this sacrifice is and accept this gift of salvation. My greatest joy is to see you and all the people I love become free from sin in Christ, leaving shame at the feet of Jesus, being transformed into His likeness, and living with purpose.

Lie #7:	I can please God by my good behavior and work.
Truth #7:	**I can only please God by faith.**

Before you move into the next chapter, reflect on the following questions:

1. Have you ever tried pleasing God with your good behavior?

2. How do you feel when you sin or make a mistake? What words would you use to describe yourself in these situations?

3. How have you separated yourself from this world to avoid sin?

4. How does the idea of sin being inside you rather than outside you change the way you think about it?

Chapter 8

He Loves Me

> *"But God demonstrates his own love for us in this: While we were still sinners, Christ died for us."*
>
> **— Romans 5:8**

Several weeks after I came back from the mission trip, I moved into an apartment with four roommates. It was cheaper for all of us to pitch in money to share a place than to live on campus. I kept myself pretty busy with school, working at the coffee shop, and doing church activities. I also found that I had some special talents. I taught myself to cut hair, which I used to practice on my four brothers, dad, and grandpa. I even cut my mom's hair, as well as some other ladies who were brave enough to let me. When I would occasionally be asked to cut someone's hair in college, I never declined. It was easy and it gave me the opportunity to stay busy, build more friendships, and give back for all the kindness I received from others. The other talent I discovered I had was writing. I took all of the creative and advanced writing classes I could in college because I always found them interesting, and people often asked me for help when they needed to write an essay. Everyone who knew me knew these were two things I did well, including my roommates, who were a cool bunch of ladies from different states who didn't have family in town. We were happy we could find each other and coordinate living together.

Living with others made it difficult to hide my eating disorder. I think the girls suspected something was not right with me but no one ever asked me about it outright. I don't even know what I would have done if they had. I desperately tried to control it, but it was a daily struggle and all I thought about throughout the day. I would wake up early with a strong conviction that I would not eat anything bad that day. I created this list of *good* and *bad* foods in my mind. Anything sweet or bready was bad, and meat and veggies were good. I went for a run every morning and would feel pretty good about myself, then I would eat a *good* breakfast and start the day feeling very much under control.

At about lunch time, I would begin getting extra hungry, so I would eat lunch. Then I would continue craving more food as the day kept going, so I'd look for snacks. If there weren't any healthy snacks, I'd give in to comfort food. Once I'd crossed over and eaten something on my *bad* list, which was forbidden for me, I would get upset at myself, and to make myself feel better, I would eat more of it because I knew that starting tomorrow I would need to never touch this particular food again.

Eating more would make me not only physically sick but would also begin a panic attack about how I was going to gain all this extra weight. This caused me to look for an immediate solution to my problem, which was to purge everything in the toilet. Afterward, I would feel relief for a moment, but then start feeling bloated, hungry, and lethargic. I would take a pill to fall asleep and try again the next day. Some days I actually made it through the day without purging and without pills, and I felt amazing when I was able to do that; but many days, I felt defeated and hopeless that I would ever break this cycle.

I needed professional help, but I was afraid to tell anyone about it. Just prior to moving to Fresno, I had actually reached out for help and gone for a consultation. They gave me a diet plan and not much else. They also sent my mom a bill, which raised her concerns. She asked me about it and I lied, telling her that I no longer had this problem. Since then, my problem had gotten worse and no amount of dieting was helping—it was actually making it worse.

According to the Eating Disorder Coalition, whose mission is to advance the recognition of eating disorder as a public health priority in the United States, about 30 million Americans will struggle with an eating disorder in their lifetime. Eating disorders have the second highest mortality rate of any mental illness, with someone dying every 62 minutes as a result of an untreated eating disorder.[40] If you are not familiar with eating disorders, they are mainly classified into three categories: anorexia (not eating), bulimia (binging and purging), and binge eating (overeating). I was bulimic and did not realize the severity of my problem, so I tried to control it on my own.

At the time, I wasn't looking for a relationship—It was enough trouble keeping my mask intact and pretending everything was okay. I stayed very busy to avoid downtime, which would temp me to turn to food for comfort. I still dreamed about getting married one day, having kids, and living my happily ever after, but it was hard to imagine anyone would ever want to be with me knowing my issues. I spent many nights praying about my disorder and my future husband.

It had been almost a year of living in Fresno and though there were a few guys who showed a little interest in me, I could never tell if it was because they wanted a relationship or if they were just nice, like my friend had told me. So I tried to stay neutral in terms of friendship with guys and told myself not to let anything go to my head. I was only going to be friends, nothing more.

Then, one evening, someone called our apartment and one of my roommates picked up the phone. It was a young man by the name of Vadim, who asked if anyone in our apartment could help him write a paper for English class. My roommate immediately said, "Oh, that's Nicole!" and handed me the phone. I recognized the voice on the other end of the line. A while back, he had asked me to give him a haircut, so I had cut his hair at the Russian house. That day on the phone, he asked me if I could help him write an essay on Romeo and Juliette, which would require watching the movie. Without hesitation, I agreed.

He picked me up a few days later and we were headed to his place to watch the movie. On the way, he stopped by the store and bought some vanilla ice cream—a very large bucket, actually. When we arrived at his place, his sisters were at home, but I don't remember his parents being there. He started the movie and sat on the other couch across from where I was sitting. As the movie was playing, his sisters came by and got some ice cream, putting it in little cups that were sitting on the coffee table. I loved melted ice cream around the edges of the bucket, so I picked up a spoon and just ate straight out of the bucket, not thinking anything of it because I really didn't care what he or his sisters thought of me. I was there to do business and write the paper.

After we watched the movie, I went into the bathroom and threw up all the ice cream I'd eaten. This was how sick I was with the disorder. Then, as if nothing happened, I helped him create an outline of the paper, and told him to write the draft.

About a week later, he called me and asked if we could meet about the paper. I agreed so that I could see where he was at and help him with the next step. He picked me up and we went to Olive Garden, which I thought was a little too fancy for a tutoring session, but I didn't complain. That was one of my favorite places to eat.

When we were seated at our table, before the server could take our order, I asked him to show me what he had, as far as writing. He seemed to pretend he didn't hear me, so I waited a little longer. The waiter got our drinks and our order and left. This time I asked him a little louder and said, let's see what you got. He looked around and said I was being a little too loud. I was somewhat offended but quieted down. We got our food and I asked again, now realizing that he did not bring anything with him. So we just talked about what he could write, with me suggesting that it might be easier for me to just write the paper myself.

A few days later, he was happy to pick up the finished paper and was pleased that I went above and beyond to help him. He explained that he struggled with English because he had recently immigrated from Moldova, and then it made sense why he had been taking his time with writing.

As I was finishing my shift at the coffee shop the next day, I was surprised to see him show up and ask me if I needed help with anything. I thought maybe he was paying me back for the paper since I had not charged him anything for my writing. I figured this was a good exchange of services, telling him he could pick up all of the chairs, sweep the floor, and take out the trash. I was impressed when he agreed. Once we were finished, he waited till I closed the shop, making sure I got into my car before he left. I really appreciated the gesture because it was always scary to close by myself at the end of the night.

The next day, he came back again, and I welcomed his help. He would call first to ask me if I needed help, and I would always say, "I think I'm fine," but he would still show up; I didn't mind. He kept coming to help me close. I thought it was already enough of a payment for the paper, yet he still came. I continually asked myself, *Why is he doing this? Could it be that he likes me? But I don't deserve anyone to like me. I'm a mess and I can't fix myself. If he really knew me, he'd stop coming.*

When Vadim came to spent time with me at work, he sat at the bar table right where I made drinks. He seemed like a nice guy with his big beautiful eyes, but I was not attracted to him, at least not the way I thought I should be. Don't get me wrong, he was very nice, caring, interesting to talk to, had a sense of humor, and a gentleness about him that I liked, but I couldn't say I liked him more than a friend. After all, I was afraid to like anyone at that time. I knew nobody would want to be with someone like me, if they knew the real me.

On November 17, 2001, all of our church youth went somewhere out of town, and I stayed back. As I was driving out of the parking lot after church, somewhat disappointed that all my friends were gone, I saw Vadim walk toward my car. I rolled down the window and he asked me if I had any plans that day. I was actually looking for plans, since Sundays were usually days when youth would get together and go places, so I told him I wanted to do something and was open to anything.

He offered to go to the mall. I thought it was a good idea because I was looking for a coat, since it started getting cold. We left my car near the church, and I went in his vehicle, which was a borrowed car from his uncle. We spent a few hours going from store to store looking for my coat. When I finally found exactly what I wanted, it was fairly expensive, and I thought maybe I would wait to buy it, but he offered to get it for me. I accepted and told him I would pay him back.

After the mall, we went to get some coffee at a French bakery, where he bought me a latte and a pastry—my favorite. It felt like a sweet little date except we weren't dating. I remember thinking, as he dropped me back at the church by my car, *I have not had a nice date like this for a long time.* It felt good and he asked if maybe we could do it again. I said that would be nice. After all, I still owed him money for the coat.

A few weeks later, on one of the evenings after we closed the shop, he asked me if I wanted to go somewhere. I wasn't sure what he had in mind, so I suggested a movie theater. I went home and got dressed, putting on my high heeled boots and the coat he'd bought me. Instead of the theater, he took me to a golf course, which was the nicest place in Fresno at that time. If you have never been to Fresno, it is a small town compared to big cities like Seattle or Los Angeles, so if you wanted to go on a date, you would either go to a movie, a park, or a restaurant. Or you can take a walk on the golf course, which is where he took me.

I felt a little strange going with him because I didn't know where this was going to lead. Thus far we were just friends and I was not sure it could be anything else, but I felt he wanted more. As we walked down the little trail that night, he started telling me about how he didn't just come to put up chairs and clean the floors at my coffee shop, that he came to see me. I knew at some point he would say that, but I was not ready to respond. I did not have those strong feelings that I knew I was supposed to have. I didn't love him. Yes, he was nice, actually very nice, and I really did want to like him like that, but it was just not there, and I couldn't force the feeling. Besides, I was wearing my high heels and he was walking on the lower side of the trail, looking like he was a whole head shorter than me. He was dark and handsome, but not tall. As I looked his way, I kept thinking, *This will never work. I am way too tall for him.* I kept quiet, not knowing what to say.

I went home that night and I got on my knees and prayed. I told God that if this was the man I was supposed to marry, then give me love. I wanted to love him the way he loved me. I went to bed that night and God had answered my prayer. Something changed in how I saw him and I couldn't wait to see him the next day; with each day that passed after that, my love toward him grew. We started seeing each other every day. He bought a car, which had been my dream car ever since I was a young girl, and I felt like he bought it for me. In reality, he had—it was for us.

Things were going well. I was finishing another year of college and getting ready to go on another mission trip. The group going on this trip had some of the same people, but there were new people joining as well. It was exciting to go back to see the same kids from last year because they had begged us to adopt them, so we knew they were waiting for us.

This time though, the trip felt different, probably because I felt like someone was waiting for me when I returned. During these five weeks that I was gone, I had a lot of time to think about our relationship. I also had my eating disorder completely in control, and actually lost twenty pounds. I couldn't believe this man loved me, and his love was transforming my life. I wondered if everything would change if he knew about my secrets but was hoping and praying that it wouldn't.

When I came back after the trip, there was a bouquet of flowers waiting for me in my apartment. I was so happy to see him. We took a walk and I shared the highlights of the trip and some of the miracles I had seen, as well as how much I missed him. The test of time over the mission trip confirmed that I was indeed in love with Vadim and he with me.

One evening, as he was dropping me off in my apartment, he asked me the question I knew would certainly come up one day. He asked if I had been with anyone. I knew exactly what he meant, and I felt like this could be it and our relationship would end. *Why would he want to be with someone like me?* Fearing that my secret could be discovered, I asked him to keep this between us, regardless of what happened. He promised it would and I answered *yes* to his question.

He didn't ask anything else, but was quiet for some time, processing what I had said. I think I even saw his eyes water a little, though he was pretty good about hiding emotions. At this awkward silence, I didn't know what to do, whether to leave or stay. I was ready for the worst-case scenario but hoped for the best. I thought even if he did leave me, it felt good to release even that one word from my shame-weary soul. The secret tortured me and being able to tell this one person a little tiny bit of it made it feel as though a whole boulder fell off my shoulders. Someone else knew about my past and they hadn't run yet.

After a few minutes of silence, he said that he didn't want to know anything, nor did he want this subject to ever come up in our relationship. *What's past is past.* I didn't expect him to just move past it so quickly, but I was glad he did. I did not want to talk about the past and I was happy he'd said he would never bring it up. I felt like another boulder had fallen off my shoulders. I felt a thousand times lighter.

That night I learned a valuable lesson about grace. Vadim demonstrated grace toward me by accepting me—imperfect. If he had left, I would have deserved it and I would have completely understood. But when he didn't leave me, I felt accepted even though he knew one of the worst things I've done. *This is love.* And it was so good to finally get that off my chest and begin my journey to freedom.

What is important to grasp here is that love has the power to transform a person. The reason I included all of the elements of our relationship in this book is because I wanted to show how undeserving I was of his love. Not only did I have a deeply sinful past, I was also struggling with an eating disorder. The love I received from Vadim wasn't enough to fully understand God's grace and love for me, but it was the beginning of that understanding.

God loves us just the same, with all of our biggest sins and with those dysfunctional behaviors. Romans 5:8 says, "But God demonstrates his own love for us in this: While we were still sinners, Christ died for us." God loves you in your sins and in your pain. He hates to see you struggle and wants to heal you, but the only way to be healed of our dysfunction is to believe that He loves us fully and completely, in all our mess. Not only the mess we made in the past, but the mess we make now, and all the mess we have yet to make. Psalm 103:3-5 never gets old, "[He] who forgives all your sins and heals all your diseases, who redeems your life from the pit and crowns you with love and compassion, who satisfies your desires with good things so that your youth is renewed like the eagle's."

This is unconditional love—love that does not depend on anything you have done or will ever do. No matter how messy our lives are and how much pain we have caused ourselves and others, His love is constant toward us. We know that because God is love. Jeremiah 31:3 says, "I have loved you with an everlasting love; I have drawn you with unfailing kindness."

I can see how my life was similar to the Israelites, who continued to rebel against God, yet He continued to love them and fight for them. They complained about the hardships and grumbled about daily provisions, which God provided for them. They were quick to get angry because they didn't trust God, who as a matter of fact, had just parted the Red Sea, which all of them walked through. This is what you call unconditional love. They grumbled, complained, showed their angry attitude, which just demonstrated their lack of faith, yet God still gave them what they needed and quenched their thirst.[41]

Well if that wasn't enough, they continued to grumble, but then it was about food. These Israelites were telling God that they would go back to slavery and die there rather than trust God, just because they didn't get what they wanted; they were basically having a temper tantrum.[42] In other words, they did not think God was able to provide for them and meet their needs.

But it didn't end there. The Israelites continued to rebel and make God angry when they asked Aaron to make them a golden calf after Moses was gone on the mountain receiving the 10 commandments. And you know what happened then? God wanted to wipe them from the face of the earth and create a whole new nation from Moses. However, Moses interceded on their behalf and God relented. He could have easily destroyed them, but because of an intercessor, they remained alive.[43]

The lesson here is that God is a holy God and He demands perfection. Just like the nation of Israel, we continue to rebel against God in our grumbling, complaining, anger, and us running to our own idols and desires. All because of our lack of faith. Yet, He continues to provide for us and take care of our needs. And even in moments when His righteous anger burns, there is an intercessor, by the name of Jesus, who is advocating for us, just like Moses interceded on behalf of the Israelites. God poured out His wrath on Jesus Christ on the cross who died on our behalf and now sits at the right hand of God to intercede for us. Hebrews 7:25 tells us, "Therefore he is able to save completely those who come to God through him, because he always lives to intercede for them." Jesus was brutally beaten, spit upon, and mocked, but as He hung on the cross, he said, "Father, forgive them, because they do not know what they are doing" (Luke 23:34). He interceded while hanging on the cross. Jesus continues to intercede for us as long as He lives, which we know is forever. That is unconditional love.

Vadim showed me unconditional love in how he pursued me, even though I was in my sin and completely unworthy of his love. But his love compelled me and transformed me in a way that ensured I was able to begin healing not only from my past, but from my struggles with my eating disorder. If that is what human love can do, it is beyond comprehension to what God's love can do.

This is how much God loves you! No matter how much you continue to deny Him and rebel against Him, He is actively pursuing you, waiting until you put your faith in Him. And when you do, you will not only experience joy, peace, and an abundance of hope, but your life will be transformed so that you can live by the power of His love, walking in your God-given purpose, instead of living for yourself.

Experiencing unconditional love from Vadim allowed me to see myself in a different light. I started viewing myself as lovable, beautiful, and desirable. When I believed I had value, I started treating myself better, though all of this happened on a subconscious level.

I don't know your situation, but I do know that your unwanted habits and behaviors are rooted in your identity, of who you believe you are. Notice how you talk about yourself and how you talk to people around you. The self-talk you use for yourself gives you a window into your belief system. That belief system will either bring life or death into your existence. That belief system will also affect other people because we tend to project our beliefs onto other people. When you stop believing that God's love depends on your behavior and embrace the truth about His unconditional love, you will experience transformation.

Lie #8:	God's love is conditional and depends on my behavior.
Truth #8:	**God's love is constant and does not depend on my behavior.**

Before you move into the next chapter, reflect on the following questions:

1. Describe a time you experienced positive change in yourself because someone demonstrated unconditional love toward you.

2. Is there someone (or more than one person) in your life who needs your unconditional love demonstrated toward them? List their name(s).

3. What can you do to demonstrate love toward them?

Chapter 9

Saved by Grace

> *"I have loved you with an everlasting love; I have drawn you with unfailing kindness. I will build you up again, and you, Virgin Israel, will be rebuilt."*
>
> **— Jeremiah 31:3-4**

Vadim and I got engaged exactly one year after our first unofficial date (the night he bought me the coat, which, by the way, I never paid him back for). He took me to Olive Garden for the anniversary dinner, and this time I did not embarrass him with loudly asking questions about his paper. We were there for a nice date. He excused himself multiple times during dinner and I was a little curious as to what was happening to him. But then came desert with a ring on the side.

I was glad it wasn't inside the desert because I never liked those kinds of proposals. I was surprised but had wanted something to happen on this anniversary. We were both old enough for a serious relationship. I had just turned twenty-two and he was twenty-four. When I saw the ring, I gasped because, for one, I was surprised, but two, I was happy that he finally made the decision to propose. He didn't get on one knee, which I kind of wanted, but it would have drawn way too much attention in the restaurant, so I was okay with how he did it. He just asked, "Would you be my wife?" I looked at him, looked back at the ring, looked back at him, and answered, "Yes!" It was a beautiful moment and it felt amazing to say *yes* to someone I truly loved.

We got married on May 24, 2003, in Tacoma, Washington. My parents played a huge role in helping us plan and even pay for the wedding. I lived in Fresno and was in my last semester before graduating college. I could not leave until after the graduation, which was about three weeks before our wedding. We made our own invitations in an effort to save a little money, since we didn't have much money to start a family. Thankfully Vadim had just accepted a job at a hospital two months before the wedding. I was planning to get my teaching credential after we got married, so it was amazing that he had a stable job that could provide for both of us while I was still at school.

The wedding was beautiful with colors of light gold and white. We had a band from Spokane and two of our friends led the reception with humor and tact. It was a typical Slavic wedding. First was the ceremony and Vadim looked like a ghost because he hardly got any sleep—he had spent the whole morning trying to find his best men, who came from out of town and didn't know the address of where they were staying. (Obviously, this was before iPhone maps existed). Of course, he also hadn't eaten anything, and hadn't been feeling good since morning. I thought he was going to faint because he rocked back and forth as the pastor kept speaking. He was clearly relieved when it was finally the prayer and *kiss the bride* part.

At the reception, we were relaxed. I prepared to lip sync a song for Vadim, which was supposed to be a surprise. I always loved how brides would sing at weddings to their groom or vice versa. And since I was not a singer, I thought I could at least pretend to be one. I stood far away from him so he would not hear my actual voice. I sounded really good until he started coming closer and noticing that it wasn't my voice. I tried to push him away so he would not give it away to the audience, but they figured it out. I learned I could never be fake with Vadim, and in that case with anyone else because eventually the truth comes out.

At the end of the celebrations, after unwrapping the gifts at our parents' house, Vadim's best man dropped us off at our hotel, which was beside the airport, because the next morning we were supposed to fly out to our honeymoon in Honolulu, Hawaii. I remember getting ready for our first night as husband and wife. I went to the bathroom and freshened up. When I came out, he was completely asleep on the bed. I was a little disappointed; after all, who falls asleep on their wedding night?

But I knew he was exhausted, and since we had to get up in a few hours, and I was tired myself, I fell asleep quick.

The next morning—or more like three hours later—we were on our way, flying to Hawaii just the two of us. I remember how freeing it felt to finally be together without having to tell anyone about our whereabouts. Life was great and we were happy. As we were pulling up to our hotel, I asked Vadim whether we should have kids right away or wait. I wanted him to say *right away*, but he said *later*. I was a little disappointed because I wanted to know if I would ever be able to have kids.

All my life, I was taught that there were consequences for my sins, and that I would be punished one way or another. I kind of expected God to punish me by not allowing me to have kids, though I really wanted them. If I couldn't have kids, I would know this was my punishment for my past. Not only that, but now I was facing a double punishment.

You see, when I met Vadim, I wanted to do everything right and be sexually pure until the wedding day. However, we failed in this area. Though we both grew up in Christian families and had both been baptized, our lives were full of secrets, which we would each only learn further into our marriage. We were two sinners marrying in the context of the church because that was the acceptable thing to do, yet we were both struggling with understanding salvation.

Vadim thought that if he got close to God, he would die. The reason for that was because whenever someone died young, people would say that person was ready. He felt that getting close to God meant telling God that you were ready to go to heaven, so he was a "Christian" at a distance; he went to church, followed all the rules, but his heart wasn't transformed by an intimate relationship with God. He used to steal, drink, and go to clubs, but had to be in church on Sunday morning, no exception. He was just religious, which was really easy to do in a church that focused more on external appearance and behavior, rather than transformation of the heart. When we got married, he actually insisted that I wear a head covering to church. He expected his wife to look like a real church girl, cute head covering included. At the same time, he wanted me to wear a short skirt because he said long skirts made me look like a grandma. I tried to be an obedient wife.

After a few Sundays of me struggling with trying to put on this head covering, which didn't sit right on my short hair, he gave up. He told me he didn't really care. At that time in our church, women were supposed to wear head coverings, but if their husband allowed them not to, it was acceptable. I was happy about that because I never understood why women needed it. It says in 1 Corinthians 11:15 that your hair serves as covering, "For long hair is given to her as a covering." My husband, though he wanted to appear religious and had repented and been baptized, was not a born-again regenerated Christian. He knew about God but did not have a personal relationship with Him.

I remember when we got married, he asked me if I wanted to watch porn together. I was appalled. I had absolutely no desire to do that. I did not know he struggled with that at the time and it upset me a great deal that he would watch it. However, he didn't quiet see how that was hurting me. He said it should not be affecting me since he loved me and porn was nothing. He could stop it at any time.

I too had my sin struggles that continued into marriage. Most people think that getting married should take care of any struggles with sexual sin. Except it isn't that simple. And if you have ever struggled sexually, you know exactly what I mean. Having any type of addiction or unhealthy habit is only a symptom of the problem. It is important to take a deeper look at what is causing the symptom or addiction.

Both of us said we felt like we could control both of our sexual struggles, yet we could not stop it completely. As my husband described recently, he used to think of it as something you just cover with a shelf. You pretend it isn't there because it is covered by something, but when you need it, you move the shelf and it's right there. You have control over it, at least that's what you think. However, the reality is, it controls you. When you feel strong emotions or feel bored or lonely, it is usually the shelf that gets moved out of the way to access your comfort object.

With our struggles hidden from each other and from everyone else, we continued to live like nothing was ever wrong. We went to church, prayed before bed, and did our diligence in reading the Bible. But everything was at a surface level with a theoretical understanding, not a true heart transformation, so we both felt like something was missing.

We got pregnant with our first daughter three months after the wedding. I had just started my credential program and was staying busy with schoolwork. Just a week after completing my credential, on our first-year anniversary, I delivered my first-born daughter, Alena. It was a dream come true for me. I had always dreamed about having a baby and was so pleased that God had mercy on me and given me a child.

A year later, I started my first teaching job and soon found out I was pregnant with my second child. I was only working part time, but the job was demanding because it was an intervention class for students with behavioral and academic challenges. The hardest part was when my principal, who had never visited my class, gave me a bad evaluation. She was unkind in her interactions with me, or lack thereof, and for some reason she felt like I was not a good teacher, though I went above and beyond.

This crushed me because I've been practicing being a teacher all my life. I used to put all of the kids that came to our house behind desks and play school. I taught Russian school, Sunday school, led kids' camps, went on mission trips where I worked with kids, organized a whole Russian school, and now I'd been deemed incapable of teaching. My teaching pride plummeted. I had experienced another version of rejection and I felt like a failure. I'd failed in my personal life and now I had failed in my professional life.

I had worked so hard for this career, trying to earn good grades all my life, going to college early, getting a higher education, getting my credential, passing all the impossible tests, and finally when I reached my career, I failed. It hurt and it hurt bad. Not only that, but we had just bought a house. We had mortgage to pay and Vadim was not working full time. Thankfully, I connected with a Christian mentor who supported me. She was a former administrator, who retired and began working as a support for first- and second-year teachers. She was the reason I got through this difficult time of my life, teaching me about FROG, which stands for Fully Rely On God, which I used often to remind myself to stop trying to take matters into my own hands.

All summer I searched for another job. After thirteen interviews in the same district, I gave up, saying I would just go back to substituting if I had to. After I made that decision, I spent the rest of that summer focusing on my babies and building friendships with other couples with small kids.

In August, by a supernatural miracle, and with just one interview, I got a job in a different district, one I knew nothing about. God blessed me with a job that was beyond what I expected. Everyone who came in my classroom praised me for my teaching abilities, which made me so confused as to why the first principal had failed me. But I just saw it as a blessing from God, which strengthened my faith as I fully relied on Him.

Things were looking better. I had a job and my career wasn't over. I was feeling better about myself, but still, something was not right. I didn't have peace. I was happy but not completely happy. Though I was married to a great man whom I loved, and we had two beautiful baby girls, I often felt lonely. My husband filled my needs most of the time, but not completely. My kids filled my needs most of the time, but not completely. My friends filled my needs, but not completely. My job filled my needs, but not completely. I was still searching for more. I was not sure what I needed, but when I was alone, I would feel a longing for something that I couldn't identify.

Going to church Sunday after Sunday and sitting in the baby room kept me feeling spiritually empty. We did not have a baby room where we could leave kids and attend the service in peace, so each parent had to watch their own child. It was almost impossible to focus on the sermon and attend to kids at the same time. Besides, there were other moms who were eager to talk, and majority of the time, it was a nice social hour.

During the week, I was trying to read the Bible but the same thing happened as before. I felt like it was giving me superficial power. If I read the Bible in the morning, I had a better day. So I read it for that purpose, very begrudgingly. However, I didn't understand how to read it differently. My husband and I never read together. We had tried praying together but it felt awkward, so we never did it again. It was something we did on our own, individually. The times that we would try to pray together would be with the kids and it felt very mechanical, similar to how it was when I was a kid.

I continued to be tormented by my past, and the guilt and shame that came with that. I wanted to be free, but it was hanging over my head as if a dark ghost was following me around. Sitting in church only made it worse because I wanted to be free, but the idea felt impossible. If I was a non-Christian, it would be great news, and I could go repent. But I was a struggling Christian, who couldn't get it together and fix myself, and going up to repent couldn't fix me.

I grew more depressed until one day, I decided to go to another church for a change. It's not that there was anything wrong with my church, but the routine of getting dressed for service and sitting in the baby room wasn't exciting for me. I told my husband about it, but he said he did not want to go to another church, especially an American church. He felt like our church was the only church that was holding on to the truth and he couldn't trust another church. So, I went by myself.

I remember sitting down with no one paying much attention to me. Everything felt casual there—the way people dressed, the way they interacted—and I felt comfortable. When the pastor came out to preach, he was smiling and joking around. It was unusual for me to see a pastor happy behind a pulpit. He opened the Bible and started speaking in very simple terms that I could understand. It sounded like everyday language, instead of technical Biblical language. He was also so excited about what he was preaching, that I was listening to him with an open mouth. Everything he said penetrated my heart like water penetrating thirsty soil. I was gulping it down as if I hadn't drunk in twenty years. Everything he said spoke to me and the encouragement I felt ignited a fire in my soul.

I came home glowing with hope. I couldn't stop talking about how amazing the sermon was, how excited the pastor was, and how caring the people were. They announced that after church, if you were a woman who needed an oil change, there were men who could help. I think it must have been Mother's Day or something. I can't remember exactly, but I thought that was a really neat way to serve. If I were single, I would have definitely appreciated that offer.

My husband was a little suspicious about what this church was doing when I mentioned this offer to single women, so he decided to join me the following Sunday. We took both of our kids and were able to leave them in childcare, which was an absolute gift to a mom who had spent the last three years in the baby room watching kids. I wondered if that was the reason why I felt so spiritually empty. Regardless of the reason, I was happy to sit in church with my husband without kids. We could actually listen and focus.

Vadim left the service that day with a whole new perspective on this church. He told me he understood everything the pastor was saying, and it made sense to him in a practical way. We continued attending this church for the next seven years, though the first two years, we were just consumers. We just wanted to grow spiritually and get a break from our kids. I was so grateful for all those ladies that volunteered in the nursery and took care of my babies so we could actually sit in church.

Though I was growing spiritually, I still struggled with thoughts about my past. I never felt complete freedom from the guilt and shame. I desired to be in a community of people who could understand me. One summer, our church ladies in the Russian church gathered together for a program called *The Wisdom for Mothers* by Denise Glenn. It was amazing to be around women who were in similar circumstances in life. These were young moms with kids. It was the first time I connected with Slavic women on a more personal level.

When the program ended, so did the weekly meetings, and I felt a sense of loneliness again. I had just had my third child, and all my family lived in a different state, so I could not turn to them for support. My feelings of loneliness were only growing.

I tried to read more of the Bible and grow spiritually, but I still found myself severely depressed. Then I learned about a program called *Bible in 90 Days*. I was skeptical of it at first, when my sister-in-law told me that their church was going through it. I remember saying that it was impossible to read the Bible in ninety days. But that night I went on their website and learned that if I read twelve to sixteen chapters a day, I would read the entire Bible in eighty-eight days.

Though I grew up in a Christian home, I struggled with reading through the entire Bible, often getting stuck in the middle and skipping to the New Testament. I also struggled to grow spiritually, never really feeling any spiritual power from reading. I felt like it was an impossible task and, considering my past attempts, knew I could not read it on my own. Thus, I invited all the ladies I met in *The Wisdom for Mothers* program to read with me. About twenty of them agreed to read and meet weekly for discussions and videos. At the end of ninety days, twelve of us completed the entire program, with some of us reading the entire Bible for the very first time.

And to my great amazement, it was through the passages in the Bible that I always skipped that the Holy Spirit finally got a hold of my heart and revealed to me the grace I so desperately needed, though this was only the beginning of my understanding. The following verses were written to the nation of Israel, God's chosen people, who kept rebelling against the Lord, yet He continued to show His everlasting love, and I saw myself there:

"Fear not, for I have redeemed you; I have summoned you by name; you are mine" (Isaiah 43:1).
"Return, faithless Israel... you have scattered your favors to foreign gods under every spreading tree..." (Jeremiah 3:12-13).
"Return, faithless people; I will cure you of backsliding" (Jeremiah 3:22).
"I have loved you with an everlasting love; I have drawn you with unfailing kindness. I will build you up again, and you will be rebuilt, Virgin Israel" (Jeremiah 31:3-4).
"The Lord your God is with you, he is mighty to save. He will take great delight in you; he will quiet you with his love, he will rejoice over you with singing" (Zephaniah 3:17).

I never saw the story of Israel as my own story. This was a profound understanding for me. This was a nation whose people were chosen by God, who had seen firsthand what God did, when He took them out of the land of slavery, who provided for them day and night while they walked through the wilderness for forty years, who brought them into the promised land and blessed them. Yet, they kept walking away, turning to their own idols, and trusting their own strength.

Well, what do you know? I was doing the same thing. I was a slave to sin, yet He rescued me, had showed me so many miracles and given me so many blessings, walked me through the wilderness of my life, yet this whole time, I kept turning away by trusting in my own strength. I didn't fully understand the extent of God's love for me. No matter how many times Israel had walked away and scattered her favors, God was waiting for her to return, because only with Him could she completely experience the love, peace, and joy she so desperately wanted.

All God wanted me to do was to stop trying to fix myself on my own, to stop trying to be perfect and never sin, to stop trying to save myself, and to return to him, who could save me, take away my disgrace, and heal me. This was the first time I felt like I knew God with my heart, not just my head. I was so focused on pleasing God with my works, my behavior, and my accomplishments, but all He wanted was my heart, as broken as it was. I was worried about what other people thought more than what He thought of me. I was letting my shame control my life and take away my peace and joy.

God is a compassionate God who is ready to receive you. All He wants is your wandering heart. He is actively pursuing you. All my Bible reading throughout my life was a religious duty that I did out of guilt. I thought by reading and memorizing verses I could somehow save myself, but it was a dead religion. What saved me was when I started believing the truth written in the Bible, that God provided a solution for my guilt and shame, which is found in a relationship with God Himself.

God is not interested in me memorizing facts about Him, but He wants me to know Him. Jeremiah 9:23-24 records the words of the Lord, "Let not the wise boast of their wisdom or the strong boast of their strength or the rich boast of their riches, but let the one who boasts boast about this; that they have the understanding to know me, that I am the Lord, who exercises kindness, justice and righteousness on earth." In order to know God, I had to give up trying to work on my sin, trying to cover up my shame, and trying to do religious activity for the sake of feeling better about myself.

After I understood the extent of God's love for me, even in the midst of my struggles with sin, my hope was renewed, and I started reading God's word, not out of guilt and duty, but out of my desire to know Him. I read it over and over again and could not get enough of it. I have marked up Bible after Bible, from one translation to another. I could not go a day without reading, not because I needed to meet a reading quota or overcome my sin struggle, but because I could not wait to hear what the Lord was going to tell me each day. It felt like the Bible all of a sudden came alive. I am sure that it was always alive, but it was not reviving me, which was because I had not accepted the truth. John 8:31-32 records Jesus's words as He spoke to the Jews, "If you hold to my teaching, you are really my disciples. Then you will know the truth, and the truth will set you free."

The Jews responded that they had never been enslaved to anyone since they were Abraham's children,[44] but Jesus answered them, "I tell you the truth, everyone who sins is a slave to sin. Now a slave has no permanent place in the family, but a son belongs to it forever. So if the Son sets you free, you will be free indeed. I know you are Abraham's descendants. Yet you are ready to kill me, because you have no room for my word" (John 8:34-37).

These Jews knew the word of God, but it did not transform their lives, because the word of God is Jesus Himself. These Jews did not accept Jesus, so their entire religion was fruitless. Until I accepted Jesus and the grace He offered, without me having to prove anything, I was reading the Bible without transformation. In order for any transformation to occur, I had to accept that I was powerless to change myself, stop my sins, and do what He wanted me to do. Oh, I tried, and I tried for a long time, but it only wore me out. It felt like I was running on a treadmill, doing all these things, trying so hard to be good, to please God, to please others, and at the end of the day, I was still not enough.

Unless you can fathom the extravagant gift of God's grace, you will continue trying to live by your own effort and no amount of reading and serving will ever make you good enough because, at the end of the day, you will still miss the mark. So let go of your fruitless efforts of trying to do these religious duties to earn favor or prove to yourself that you are a Christian, trying to work for God, serving to earn favor with people and God, and trying to live a perfect life to feel better about yourself, while falling short every time. Once you let go and let God transform you, walking in His Spirit, knowing His heart, and following wherever He takes you, then you will experience the true freedom and joy that come from a relationship with God. Philip Yancey defines grace like this:

"Grace means there is nothing we can do to make God love us more—no amount of spiritual calisthenics and renunciations, no amount of knowledge gained from seminaries and divinity schools, no amount of crusading on behalf of righteous causes. And grace means there is nothing we can do to make God love us less—no amount of racism or pride or pornography or adultery or even murder. Grace means that God already loves us as much as an infinite God can possibly love."[45]

Can you imagine this? It is difficult to grasp. This is grace. When a person is saved, and genuinely understands this truth, that person wants to do what their heavenly Father wants them to do. The reason why Christian people still sin is because they are still living in a sinful body that will continue experiencing temptations. However, they have peace about their eternity because nothing they do will alter it. That is the peace that gives people security, which releases the bonds of shame, making it possible to turn away from the destructive patterns we use to cope with shame. If you have grasped this truth, you have probably experienced your chains falling off. If you haven't, I hope you do soon.

When my husband demonstrated unconditional love and I received it, I recovered from my eating disorder. When God revealed to me His unconditional love and I received it, I was healed from my sexual addiction and thoughts. Not all of my sin issues got resolved immediately, but God was slowly freeing me from sins that entangled me. Freedom in Christ is essential to breaking any addiction or sin, but more importantly, it frees us to share what God has done in our lives and not be afraid of what people might think. After all, it is not our story, it is His story of grace and redemption. I hope that this book will encourage you to share your story of redemption because you just never know when it can help someone else grasp the truth of the power of God's amazing grace.

Lie #9:	Reading and memorizing the Bible will transform my life.
Truth #9:	**Believing the truth in the Bible will transform my life.**

Before you move into the next chapter, reflect on the following questions:

1. What sin struggles do you experience that you feel you have perfect control over?

2. What is your motivation for reading the Bible?

3. If you have little or no motivation to read the Bible, what are some reasons for that?

4. Have you accepted the extravagant gift of grace? What evidence of that acceptance do you see in your life?

Chapter 10

The Invitation

> *"Your story is the key that can unlock someone else's prison."*
>
> **— Billy Graham**

The ladies kept coming, though I was in no position to lead them. All I had wanted was a community to study the Bible together and grow spiritually. I never even imagined leading a woman's group because I thought I would never be worthy, especially in the Russian church. Leaders had to have demonstrated faithfulness all their lives and should be somewhat perfect so people could strive to be like them. I did not want anyone to strive to be like me. I was still a mess with so many unresolved issues and much-needed healing.

Nonetheless, because the ladies wanted to continue meeting, we started doing other studies and inviting more women. The group was growing both spiritually and in numbers, though I continued fearing that if they only knew my past, they would stop coming.

A few years into the meetings, I received an invitation from my friend Natasha to speak to young girls in Everette, Washington. She was speaking to youths and parents about sexuality God's way, and since I led a group of women, Natasha thought to ask me to speak in a small breakout session with the girls after her talk. I hesitated, but at the same time, I wanted to tell these girls so much, especially what I would have liked to hear at that age. Looking back, I know at their age, I would have loved to attend a conference where someone could speak truthfully and use words I understood when it came to relationships and sexual purity. The only word we ever heard used in church about sexual purity was *целомудрие*, or *chastity*. We just knew that we had to be chaste, but what that meant, and why that was important, the explanations were limited.

Natasha had experience working at a pregnancy center that served girls who kept their babies instead of aborting. What she had learned was their conversations immediately went to intimate topics, even though these were girls she hardly knew. And she was confused why these topics were never discussed in our church culture and why girls had to find out about these things after they had already made these choices. She wanted to encourage parents to talk to their kids about how God designed the body and the intended purpose for its design. I was invited to speak to the girls, someone else was speaking to the parents, and someone else to the guys.

Our speaker team rented a van and drove for about sixteen hours. The entire trip, I felt very uneasy about my session. I shared my discomfort with the team and told them I was afraid to speak about certain topics from my past. I explained to them that as I was preparing and typing my notes for my talk, I could not help but include some of the ugly parts of my life. After I written it, I'd allowed my husband to see my speech, and I was literally shaking as he was reading it. When he saw how terrified I was, he told me I was not ready to go there, so I deleted that part completely and said I would just stick to the theoretical aspects of my message and skip the heart issues. It was too raw for me. After all, even my husband barely knew about my past, since he never wanted it brought up.

After I expressed my concerns to the team, they assured me that God was going to help me make the right decision on what to speak about and what to withhold. Even though I deleted the information from my notes, God knew what needed to be said. I hoped that He was not going to ask me to share any of that because I was not ready at all, even though it has been over ten years since the incident.

When we reached my parents' house in Renton, I was dropped off so I could spend some time with my family, while the team had a different arrangement in Everett. During my time there, I wanted to have a conversation with my mom about what had happened to me in case I accidentally spoke about my past at my session. I figured that way, at least my parents would be first to know, since it would be weird if they had to learn it from another source.

The opportune time came when I was sitting in the living room with my mom right across me on another couch, and my younger sister on a different couch on my left. We were just casually talking, and I shared with them that I was nervous about the next day because I was afraid I was going to spill some of my secrets. My sister recognized that this was an invitation to listen and she was ready for me to share my heart, but my mom responded by saying that others don't need to know your past because it has all been forgiven by God, which completely closed the door for a conversation. I knew she did not intend to close the door to me speaking but instead wanted to protect me from exposure. After all, it has never been comfortable for her to share issues of the heart. In our culture, we don't talk about feelings, nor do we share our deep secrets; we just keep things to ourselves and don't bother others with them because it might make them see you differently or ruin your reputation. So, despite my intentions, I said nothing to anyone that night.

The next morning, I was still feeling very uneasy about my upcoming speech, so I sat down to spend a little time with God. I wanted to hear from Him about what I should do. The desire to share my past was burning inside me and ready to burst because I wanted to let these girls know what I failed to know then, but I was terrified to expose it. I wanted to keep it hidden because I didn't know what the ramifications could be after I shared. In search of some answers, I opened the book of Nehemiah, a book about the rebuilding of the wall of Jerusalem, the holy city of God, and read, "Those who survived the exile and are back in the province are in great trouble and disgrace. The wall of Jerusalem is broken down, and its gates have been burned with fire" (Nehemiah 1:3). This was how I felt at the moment, like this survivor who returned from being in exile for many years, who was now in great trouble and disgrace, with broken walls and burned gates. I needed rebuilding. I needed healing.

However, as Nehemiah started rebuilding the wall, there was great opposition from the local officials. It says in Nehemiah 2:10, "When Sanballat the Horonite and Tobiah the Ammonite official heard about this, they were very much disturbed that someone had come to promote the welfare of the Israelites." I felt as if God was taking me through a healing process for my well-being by giving me an opportunity to share my story with lessons learned about God's grace, but there was so much opposition from the enemy. The biggest one was fear. As I continued reading and praying, I got to another verse in Nehemiah 4:14 that said, "Don't be afraid of them. Remember the great and awe-inspiring Lord, and fight for your countrymen, your sons and daughters, your wives and your homes." This verse! Oh this verse was packed with power!!!

I started thinking about why I was speaking that day. Yes, it was for my own well-being, but it was also for all of my family and my friends, and anyone else who had a secret or addiction that the enemy uses to destroy their life. I did not want my daughters to experience the same pain I did. I did not want my brothers to continue turning to destructive coping strategies, nor did I want the enemy to continue using secrecy to destroy our lives. It was time to expose the enemy's tactics, and the enemy knew it, which is why all the opposition. That was exactly what was happening with these Israelites, who were rebuilding the wall to Jerusalem while at the same time fighting off their opposition.

There will always be an enemy who does not want your well-being. Because he knows if you are well, you have the capacity to help others. And this will thwart his plans that were meant to paralyze you, keep you silent, and ineffective, focused on trying to reach perfection by doing your religious duties. This is what the enemy was doing to me the last ten years (at the time), keeping me silent and ineffective. Whenever I had an idea about doing something big for God, he would quickly remind me of my worth, and I'd lower my head and say goodbye to my God-given dream.

As I finished my time with God, I had more courage to speak, but I was still afraid. When I arrived at the church building in Everette, I was more relaxed and ready for the conference. We prayed with the pastor and got some coffee while socializing with the early arrivals. As it got closer to start time, the team gathered in a circle for another prayer. As everyone took their turn praying, tears started rolling down my eyes. I was having another moment of anxiety and I could not even pray. I just cried. After the prayer, my team encouraged me to say what God wanted me to say. I was still hesitant and scared.

Natasha was first and she spoke about how sex was designed for marriage and how it's a wonderful gift when it is used in the right context for the right purpose. She used an example of a toxic chemical such as an oven cleaner. There are typically warning signs on such chemicals. If they are used in the context within which they were designed, they are extremely helpful, but if they are taken out of the context for which they were intended, they become harmful, destructive, and even deadly. She explained that this same principle applies to marriage. Sex outside of marriage is destructive, but within marriage it is a blessing, and is meant to make the marriage bonds stronger.

She also explained about hormones and how they work in the human body; how every relationship you have is like tape that sticks to a surface. For example, if you first put a piece of tape on something, it has a tendency to stick really well, but taking the tape off and re-taping it again and again will make it lose its stickiness. She explained that your body produces these hormones that help you stick to your mate, which is what is supposed to happen when you fall in love and experience intimacy with your spouse. You are supposed to wake up and forever be stuck to them. This is why breakups are so difficult, because you basically leave pieces of yourself stuck to the person you were in a relationship with. There is an invisible bond that is built between the two of you. So, it is important not to waste that stickiness on just anyone, but to wait to use it in the right context—marriage. Song of Solomon 8:4 says, "Promise me, O women of Jerusalem, not to awaken love until the time is right."[46]

I had never heard anything explained so well before when it came to relationships. As I continued to listen, I realized why I felt trapped in the relationship with the pursuer; I was able to make more sense of what had happened to me and why it had happened.

The next person who was speaking shared his testimony about how he was molested as a little boy by a man in the hospital. He shared how he kept it his secret for a long time and how this had brought so much damage. When he talked about his secrets, I thought about my own. These were secrets, just like his, maybe different in what they were, but still secrets. Secrets I wanted to keep covered, protected, unexposed. But seeing him share his past publicly and see how much God had done for him, gave me courage to share mine. I still didn't want to and was still terrified, but I felt like maybe it was something that needed to happen for my healing to begin.

When the main session was over, the participants were split into three groups, with boys in one room, girls with me, and parents in another. I found my way to the room I was supposed to be, which happened to be the cafeteria. I felt frozen. I was still scattered, not knowing where to begin, when Natasha walked in. She asked if we had started, and since we hadn't yet, Natasha prayed before I began speaking. In that moment, I felt as though someone else took over my voice because the words just starting flowing, as if I had been preparing for this story all of my life. I used my notes as a framework for the message, but my talk still went exactly in the direction I was afraid it would go. I did not hold back but just spoke the truth, and as I did, I felt another boulder fall off my chest.

When I finally finished, I realized that my niece was in the room with me. That meant I had to share this with my family. So, as my sister rushed into the cafeteria after finishing her session for parents, I quickly told her about what had happened to me, without giving her any details. In return, she surprised me by busting out a secret that I had no idea about. We were both happy to share something with each other that had been bringing so much shame into our lives.

After the conference ended, I had an opportunity to meet a number of girls who shared their struggles and secrets. I was amazed how much my message had impacted them, and it marked the beginning of a whole new journey of healing and hope for me. The freedom that comes through exposing a secret sin that brought shame and condemnation into one's life is inexplicable. But more importantly, by exposing the sins that cripple you testifies about God's grace and mercy.

I knew the next thing I had to do was share this with my family. The conference was in Everette, near my parents, for a reason. God wouldn't create an opportunity for me to be home if He hadn't wanted me to share about what God had done for me. However, I was afraid for my dad to find out, and I wondered how I could share so only my mom and siblings could hear.

As we sat around the dinner table, my siblings asked about how the conference went and what we learned. We started talking about how growing up we never had conversations about sexuality, human development, and relationships. One of my brothers expressed that he felt like the door was always closed on the subject so there was never an opportunity to go there. It was something everyone had to figure out on their own. When we asked parents about why they didn't talk to us about any of these things, my mom responded that she really didn't know how because her parents never did either. It was something she and my dad figured out on their own as well.

The conversations continued as we kept talking about our childhood experiences. My dad stepped away for a moment and my mom started sharing how when she was young, she was almost raped by a church leader. This was a man of God, supposedly, but he was a pervert who exerted control over young women. She was disgusted by that but had to keep her mouth shut because he had a noble position in church. When she shared this, I couldn't help but burst out my secret. I did not go into the details because my mom felt uncomfortable with this subject, maybe because she already suspected it from the past, maybe because she did not know what to say. She told me that she was glad it was all in the past and I was good now. I was glad too, but the past had tormented me for so long that I felt it was never left behind, but rather stayed with me all along. That day was the first time I felt it loosen its grip on me.

When I came back to Fresno, I had to tell my story to the group of ladies that met at my house for Bible study every Monday. I told them I had to share something with them that was extremely important, something I wished I had told them before, but I couldn't until this past trip to Everette, where God had begun my healing process. As I told them the whole story, unlike the short story I told my family, they listened and cried with me. I did not know how they would respond to me once I finished speaking, but I so hoped they would accept me for me. To my amazement, they did not condemn me, nor judge me, but showed me overwhelming grace.

Since that trip, God has given me multiple opportunities to share this story of God's grace with others. I spoke in different conference and women's retreats and the impact my testimony has on people is profound. God uses it to reach people that feel trapped in their sin and shame. When they hear that someone else had experienced similar struggles, it opens a door to their healing. So many women share similar experiences with feeling trapped by sin even though they tried to do everything they can as far as religious duties. When I shared my story with my two older daughters during a girls' retreat, my oldest accepted Jesus into her life and later, my second daughter did as well. Since then, they have been baptized and actively serve in our church in various ministries. They too have their sin struggles and I am grateful they were able to be open with me about them, giving me an opportunity to pray for them and encourage them on their journey with Jesus. My younger daughters have also accepted Jesus as their Savior and I pray that God would use all of my kids for His glory.

I have also shared pieces of my story with friends, who in return shared some of their secrets and current pain and struggles. People are more likely to share with someone who they know will understand them. I find that many people who grew up in a similar environment as me have a hard time with letting go of their past. They become terrified about the idea of exposing it, as if they still can't forgive themselves, which is why it is difficult for them to experience true freedom in Christ and grow in an intimate relationship with Jesus. By releasing your past to God and letting Him use it for His glory in spreading the gospel, we become true ministers of reconciliation. If you keep your story to yourself, nobody benefits from it. God saved you so you can bring glory to Him through your redemption story.

Your story is not really your story—it belongs to Him who has rescued you from a dominion of darkness and brought you into the kingdom of the Son He loves.[47] I am always curious as to why when people get baptized at our church, they don't share their redemption story. Isn't that the purpose of a public baptism? It says in Matthew 3:6, "Confessing their sins, they were baptized." When you share your story, you are exposing the sin and shame out into the light, so that it no longer has power over you, while at the same time proclaiming the power of Jesus's death and resurrection. As Billy Graham says, "Your story has the key that can unlock someone else's prison." Confession not only heals your heart but can also heal someone else's heart.

When Jesus healed the demon-possessed man, sending the demons into a herd of pigs, the man wanted to go with Jesus, but Jesus said to him, "Go home to your own people and tell them how much the Lord has done for you, and how he has had mercy on you" (Mark 5:19). He told him to go and share his story about what Jesus had done. It is not a story about what you have done, how many times you repented or when you were baptized, or how you now serve in the church. It is not a story about your sin and your past. It is a story about what Jesus had done for you to rescue you from your sin and shame. You can't talk about God's goodness unless you share your deepest pain and shame.

Another example we see in the Bible is the Samaritan woman at the well who used her testimony to bring many people to believe in Jesus.[48] It was not even appropriate for Jesus to talk to a Samaritan, especially a woman, but He broke all of the barriers to reach her heart. She was never the same after that, nor could she stay quiet about what she had experienced.

The book of Psalms is filled with verses about proclaiming God's goodness and righteousness. Psalm 40:9-10 stands out to me, "I proclaim your saving acts in the great assembly; I do not seal my lips, Lord, as you know. I do not hide your righteousness in my heart; I speak of your faithfulness and your saving help. I do not conceal your love and your faithfulness from the great assembly." This is what we are called to do when we experience God's transforming power in our lives. 2 Corinthians 5:18-19 says, "All this is from God, who reconciled us to himself through Christ and gave us the ministry of reconciliation: that God was reconciling the world to himself in Christ, not counting people's sins against them. And he has committed to us the message of reconciliation."

If you are in Christ, you have a message of reconciliation to share with the world. That message does not consist of you hiding your past because you are ashamed of what you have done or what has been done to you. Instead, by exposing your past and testifying about the power of God in your life, you are giving hope to those who may still be under the deadly curse of sin and shame. Your testimony is not about you, but about God's power that can take any mess and make it into a message.

If you don't have a story about how God saved you, what is holding you back today? What lies are you still believing? Do not wait until tomorrow to begin this journey because tomorrow may never come. If you want to receive this free gift, all you have to do is believe in the finished work of Jesus on the cross, accept His forgiveness, and enter into a relationship with Him. You can pray like this:

Lord Jesus, I come to You today and acknowledge that I am a sinner. I believe You died for all my sins and rose from the dead to give me eternal life. I ask You to forgive me for trusting in my own strength. I ask You to come into my heart and transform me from the inside out. I want to follow You the rest of my life. Amen.

Lie #10:	God forgave my past so there's no point sharing it with anyone.
Truth #10:	**God wants me to testify about Him through my redemption story.**

Before you move into the next chapter, reflect on the following questions:

1. What sins from your past still come up in your memory, but you are afraid to tell other people about?

2. What is holding you back from confessing? Could it be because you are still trying to rely on your own work?

3. Are there people in your life who you can minister to with your story of redemption? List their names here.

Chapter 11

God Is Good

> *"And we know that in all things God works for the good of those who love him, who have been called according to his purpose."*
>
> **— Romans 8:28**

After my testimony in Everette, God had given me so much more freedom and peace. We had our fourth baby girl and continued attending American church, while still staying connected to the Russian church by leading ladies' Bible studies at my house. My husband and I began to get more involved in different ministries in the American church, joining a couples' Bible study group and volunteering. I also started attending MOPS, which is a ministry for Mothers of

Preschoolers. I was growing in my understanding of the gospel, reading God's word with eyes that now saw the truth, which was that God had forgiven me for all my sins, even those after baptism. Not only that but I had exposed the sin that continued bringing guilt and shame, which no longer controlled me, and I could speak about God's power without this dreadful fear. However, I was still fearful of punishment on a subconscious level, but I did a wonderful job suppressing all those thoughts and emotions by focusing on being busy.

I was known for being a "super mom" at one point in my life. I was raising four girls while working full time as a teacher and going through a master's program. At the same time, I was leading weekly Bible studies and teaching Russian school two days a week. Moreover, since I was enjoying all the programs and ministries in the American church, I started bringing those ideas into the Russian church because I wanted the ladies there to have those wonderful experiences too. This led to my husband and I completely rejoining the Russian church as members and I began taking on a leadership role in women's ministry.

Among all of that, I also wanted to have another baby—I especially wanted a boy. I loved my girls, but I wanted to experience having a boy; I imagined how he would be able to help his dad when he grew up and help me when Vadim got older. Of course, a boy wasn't guaranteed, so I would have been happy with either.

Vadim, on the other hand, did not want any more children. He never imagined having more than one or two kids, and we already had four. He also thought there was very little chance we would actually end up having a boy. This subject was always painful if I ever brought it up, and it would usually go something like this: We would go out for a nice date, I would bring up the *baby* topic, he would get angry and put his foot down, I would cry, we would go home, and I would be silent for a few days. It was really hard for me to never bring up this topic because even though I was doing so much, it was basically the only thing on my mind. I wanted a baby, boy or girl, I wanted a baby. I almost felt like this baby was already with us. We would all sit together eating lunch, and I would hear someone crying in a different room. I would look around and see that we were all there. But I was the only one who heard the crying because it was all in my imagination.

Against all odds, I got pregnant. I was afraid to tell Vadim, so I decided to wait until Father's Day. It was a happy news for me, but I wasn't sure he would have felt the same. It was really difficult to keep it a secret for a few weeks, but I wanted it to be special, so I bought a gift bag and placed the pregnancy test inside with a chocolate bar and, of course, a card. When he opened it, he was a little bit taken aback, but not upset, though I knew he wasn't too happy about it. I, on the other hand, was in seventh heaven. The baby's due date was supposed to be around his birthday on February 3, or closer to Valentine's Day if, like most of my other pregnancies, I was overdue. It was going to be perfect, at least according to my plans.

Unfortunately, the next day, I went to the doctor and discovered the hard truth that I had miscarried in the early stages of pregnancy. It was hard for me to come to terms with this because I knew that Vadim would not want to have any conversations about babies again. It either had to happen as a complete surprise, or not at all. *Why couldn't this just all work out?* I asked myself.

I grieved the loss of my baby, no matter how small. I'd had my hopes up and it was the perfect timing. All my kids would be about two to three years apart, and I'd always wanted to have them all together so they could grow and be friends with each other. Vadim, however, was relieved in a way because he was currently in his bachelor's program and life was very hectic. There was definitely a strain in our relationship after the miscarriage because I felt like he got what he wanted, and I was miserable. My heart ached and my eyes watered every time I saw a baby. I visualized holding this baby in my arms and rocking him, or her, to sleep. I was bitter for not being able to have what I wanted, while at the same time thinking that maybe God had punished me for not listening to my husband and being a stubborn wife.

A little over a year passed, and I continued to grieve over not being able to have any more children. I was also still upset with my husband. In response to these feelings, one of my friends shared with me about a book she was reading called *Created to be His Help Meet* by Debi Pearl. Through this book, God had reminded me about the chain of command He set up, which is recorded in 1 Corinthians 11:3, "But I want you to realize that the head of every man is Christ, and the head of the woman is man, and the head of Christ is God."

As a wife, my main role was to be my husband's helper, not rule over him. I was convicted by this verse as I read the book, which continued stressing the fact that there was great blessing in being submissive to our husbands, not in an unhealthy, demeaning way, but in a humble Biblical manner. I remember repenting in my journal. Here is an entry dated January 11, 2015:

> *"Dear God, I come to you today and want to thank you for opening my eyes through your word! I confess my sin of not being submissive to my husband. That is your command, yet I deliberately break it by pushing my husband into agreeing to have kids. Maybe the reason he doesn't agree is because you are trying to teach me to submit. Help me Lord and not just that, but also help me find joy in submitting because it is very sad for me to think about not ever having more kids…but Lord, I don't want to have a baby and disobey your command. Help me learn to trust You more. Help me submit with joy! Amen."*

After this prayer, I found strength in the Lord to let go of my selfish desires and allow God to do what He wanted in my life. I stopped nagging my husband about kids and put all my energy into my girls, my job, and my ministry.

A few months later, God had given me an opportunity to leave the classroom and transition into a district position working with teachers, which was a dream job for me. That same year, He blessed me with a baby. I was pregnant again, which was a complete miracle, because we had not been trying to get pregnant. Vadim accepted the idea that we were, after all, going to have another baby, and I went to my ultrasound at eight weeks and the baby's heartbeat was strong. The doctor actually said that there were two sacks, but one was empty, which meant that this could have been a twin pregnancy. I had always wanted to have twins, so I was disappointed that the other sac was empty, but still so happy the other baby was growing and well.

Three weeks later, I was back for another ultrasound at eleven weeks. I wondered why they would schedule another one so soon because with my girls, I'd only had one at eight weeks and one at twenty. But I didn't question it, thinking I wanted to have more ultrasound pictures anyway.

Vadim went with me, and as usual, the nurse practitioner did the ultrasound. We were excited to see a bigger baby and get some more pictures but noticed that the nurse practitioner's face grew very concerned. She kept looking at the monitor, as though she was trying not to panic. I was now getting worried, but she stayed calm and told me she needed to send me to a specialist to take a closer look.

We left the hospital in complete disillusionment, waiting for our specialist appointment. When the time came, we went together, hoping that the nurse practitioner had overreacted. But as this ultrasound began, we could immediately tell the specialist was also concerned. I was in tears, my husband was frantic, and the medical personnel were empathetic. Once they'd finished the scan, they walked us over to another room and told us that chances were the baby was going to have Down syndrome. The baby had a two-vessel chord instead of three, an expanded bladder, and abnormal nuchal fold measurements. They told us this was not our fault and that there were options available if we wanted to terminate the pregnancy.

I was in complete shock and could not hold back my tears. My mind was racing a thousand miles an hour. *How could this happen? How do they know for sure? How could they offer termination?* They said the only way to know for sure was to take a placenta swab and send it to a lab for testing. I was not going to terminate the pregnancy, but I really wanted to know for sure, so I agreed to go through the procedure, and they did it right then and there.

I sobbed as we drove home but Vadim was silent. I wondered what was going through his mind. *Is he blaming me for all those years that I was begging to have a baby? Does he feel this is what I deserve? Does he want to just end it?* I felt like he was angry with me, and I was angry at myself.

I locked myself in my room and spent the whole evening crying out to God. I laid on the floor and sobbed hysterically. Vadim just let me be. I felt like God was punishing me for all of my sins, for all of my rebellion, and for all of my nagging. I thought this was my cross that I needed to carry the rest of my life. And

I thought I deserved it. I deserved to see my child struggle in life, which would cause me so much pain. *Is that your good plan for me, God?* No mother wants to see her child struggle, but this would be a lifetime of uncertainty, challenges, and hardship. We as parents want the best for our children. *Don't you, God, want what's best for your children?* I also thought about how this would cause a rift in our marriage. Vadim would secretly blame me for this baby's challenges. It would all be my fault and I would have to live with this the rest of my life. *God, please heal this baby, or take him!! Please, God, heal this baby, or take him!!* I prayed for healing, I prayed for peace, I prayed for wisdom.

One of my friends, whose daughter had Down syndrome, came to comfort me and pray with me that night. She understood my grief and my pain. She had gone through all of these emotions herself and came out on the other side, now encouraging others in times of trial. Her daughter is a beautiful girl now, all grown up, who brings joy to her family and the people around her. Her life was and is not without challenges and struggles, but at the same time, she has been a blessing and a gift from God. When my friend prayed for me, she gave me courage to face tomorrow, whatever it might bring. I also asked my church to pray for us and the baby as we waited for the results to come.

Two weeks later, we received the call and the doctor gave us good news—the test was negative for Down syndrome. They did want to test for other possible abnormalities, to which I gave them permission. When all the other tests came back negative, we were relieved and praised God for this miracle.

The doctor did warn us that even if all the tests were clear, there could still be something wrong with the baby, so they were going to keep an eye on me with additional appointments and ultrasounds for the rest of my pregnancy. They suspected heart abnormalities as well as other abnormalities, which kept us on our toes the whole pregnancy.

On May 27, 2016, I delivered a healthy baby boy weighing 7 pounds 11 ounces. It was a dream come true when they placed my screaming little boy on my chest. As soon as he heard my voice, he stopped crying. He was completely healthy. We praised God for His goodness and grace.

I want to pause here and talk about something really important that I learned through this process. Earlier I mentioned how I expected God to punish me for the sins I committed. When they told me my boy was going to have Down syndrome, I thought God was punishing me, when in reality, I've realized that was never His intention. Even if my son was born with Down syndrome, it would still not have been a punishment, but rather a test of faith. My faith was tested during this process and I failed the test. I did not believe in the goodness of God. This test brought out the worst in me, which helped me give that over to God.

You see, I still misunderstood some elements of God's grace and the gospel. I thought that all of my sins deserve punishment, which is absolutely true. That punishment is death, according to Romans 6:23, "For the wages of sin is death." However, Jesus died on the cross to take my punishment upon Himself and to die in my place. I am free from punishment for my sins. This misunderstanding had me living in fear all my life. I could not trust God completely because I saw Him as a punishing God, who was waiting for the right opportunity to make my life miserable. I thought I better keep trying to live as perfect a life as I could so that I could appease God to keep Him from punishing me.

I remember every time something would happen in our family, whether our car broke down, or we had to pay an unexpected bill, or a ticket, I would always search my life and even think about my husband's life to find a sin that might have caused such bad luck. Though I did not explicitly say it to my husband or even understand it myself, I was unconsciously doing this. I was afraid to do anything wrong for my fear of punishment. What this test taught me was that God is not out to punish you; He wants good for you.

He does take us through a time of trial to test and grow our faith, but even if we fail the test, He is right there to catch us. This pregnancy taught me about God's love for me. His love does not depend on my actions, but on the actions of Jesus, who was completely perfect, and took my punishment upon Himself.

Yes, there are natural consequences for sin because sin is destructive. For example, if you overeat, you will gain weight and most likely have health issues. If you drink too much alcohol, it could destroy your liver, your relationships, and maybe even your bank account. If you lie, get angry, or gossip, your relationships and career might suffer. These are all common sense, and it does not mean God is punishing you.

What's beautiful about living in Christ is that even when we sin, our salvation is secure. Not only that, but because of this truth, we are able to have self-control. Take my struggle with food, for example; by understanding the truth that I will not lose my salvation if I overeat or binge and maybe even purge, I no longer want to overeat or purge. My overeating was done on a subconscious level as a way to suppress my shame, which stemmed out of my fear of rejection. Since I know that God loves me, my husband loves me, and my friends love me, even when I don't look great, I have no need to overeat, and can actually look great. What I am saying is that, all these things can be done by faith without trying to do them on your own strength. God wants you to take all of your sin struggle to Him in faith.

God also allows trials, which may seem like a punishment, but are meant to draw us closer to Him. These trials help develop our faith and become more like Jesus. In Proverbs 3:11-12, it says, "My son, do not despise the Lord's discipline and do not resent his rebuke, because the Lord disciplines those he loves, as a father the son he delights in." I work with teachers and we often talk about the word *discipline* because it is often equated with the word *punishment*. However, true discipline is meant *to teach* a student how to make good decisions. If a student gets kicked out of class for saying bad words, it does not teach the student anything, except that he/she now knows exactly how to get out of class and is now angry with the teacher, and maybe even planning retaliation.

However, if a student is given the opportunity to talk to the teacher, that student might learn something, and the relationship will be restored. The purpose of God's discipline is to draw us into a conversation with Him and reveal to us the issues of our heart that still need cleansing. Through my trial, I learned that I still had doubts about God's goodness to me. The sin of doubt is a serious sin that could cause damage in our lives. When we go through trials, we should never feel like we've been thrown out of class. Instead, the trial should remind us to talk to our heavenly Father who cares for us and wants to sanctify us.

Because when you stop expecting punishment, you will stop living in fear. 1 John 4:18 says, "There is no fear in love. But perfect love drives out fear, because fear has to do with punishment. The one who fears is not made perfect in love." Once you understand that your debt for your sins has been paid on the cross, eliminating all punishment, you will start seeing Christ's death and resurrection in a different light.

When you partake in the elements during communion next time, you will do so with joy and thanksgiving, because Jesus's sacrifice not only brought forgiveness of all your sins (past, present, and future), but it also took care of the punishment you deserve for all those sins. You do not have to be humiliated in front of the church for your past, but you can freely share your past to bring God glory about His grace in your life. It is difficult to fathom what this means for me. I personally have a hard time accepting this truth and want to immediately make up and add something from my own piggy bank to help pay this debt, but my change is nothing compared to the great sacrifice of Jesus. There is nothing, absolutely nothing, you can do to pay Him back for the extravagant gift of grace. The only thing you can do is accept it, receive it, and glorify His name for it continuously by telling the whole world of His great and mighty deeds in your life.

When Jesus ascended into heaven, He told His disciples to wait for the Holy Spirit, as recorded in Luke 24:49. They waited until the day of Pentecost, which was fifty days after Jesus's resurrection. Here is what happened, "Suddenly a sound like the blowing of a violent wind came from heaven and filled the whole house where they were sitting. They saw what seemed to be tongues of fire that separated and came to rest on each of them. All of them were filled with the Holy Spirit and began to speak in other tongues as the Spirit enabled them." (Acts 2:2-4). The crowd was confused about what was going on because they heard their own language spoken even though all of these people were Galileans. It was God who gave them the ability to speak in different languages, but don't miss the most important fact here. What did they speak about? The answer is in Acts 2:11, "We hear them declaring the wonders of God in our own tongues!" What is important to note here is that these disciples were speaking about the wonders of God, or as the Christian Standard Bible says, "magnificent acts of God." They were preaching the finished work of God on the cross, which paid their ransom for their sin, their shame, and their punishment. Jesus had done the same for us. How could we be quiet about the work of God in our lives when He has done so much for us?

Whenever I have an opportunity to share the work of God in my life, just as I am sharing here through this book, I often receive feedback that goes something like this: "It makes so much sense why you are so passionate for God, why you are involved in women's ministry, and why you constantly talk about God's amazing grace. God has forgiven you so much! But for me, it is different. I have not committed any big sins. I have always been a good girl and lived a righteous life. I have never done the things you have done. This is why I can't be as passionate as you."

Have you ever thought this way when someone shared their life with you, thinking that you are much better than that person? We see a story similar to this in Luke 7:36-48, where Jesus visited a Pharisee who judged Him when a sinful woman touched Him. Jesus then used a scenario about two debtors who owed different amounts of money with one owing five hundred denarii and the other fifty. Neither one of them could pay it back and both debts were canceled. Who would love the creditor more?[49] It is logical that the one who owed more would love Him more, which was the Pharisee's response. This is what Jesus said to the Pharisee, "Do you see this woman? I came into your house. You did not give me any water for my feet, but she wet my feet with her tears and wiped them with her hair. You did not give me a kiss, but this woman, from the time I entered, has not stopped kissing my feet. You did not put oil on my head, but she has put perfume on my feet. Therefore, I tell you, her many sins have been forgiven—as her great love has shown. But whoever has been forgiven little loves little" (Luke 7:44-47).

You might look at this example and say, this makes sense. The Pharisee is more righteous than the woman, which is what I hear when people tell me how they don't have much sin to be forgiven compared to me. This might be completely true, according to human standards; however, the bigger problem was that this Pharisee was blind to his own sin and failed to see himself as a sinner. Read the previous verses again and observe all the things the Pharisee didn't do, as compared to the woman. James 4:17 says, "If anyone, then, knows the good they out to do and doesn't do it, it is sin for them." All those things were customary to do when you had a guest in the Jewish tradition. The bigger lesson to take away here is about our own acknowledgment of sin. If we claim to have not sinned because we had attempted to live a moral life, we become this Pharisee. 1 John 1:8-9 says, "If we claim to be without sin, we deceive ourselves and the truth is not in us. If we confess our sins, he is faithful and just and will forgive us our sins and purify us from all unrighteousness."

Here is the key: confession or acknowledgment of sin, which requires humility, is essential for salvation. If we claim that we haven't sinned that much, which might be true, as compared to other people, we still miss the mark. Any sin, as small as not doing what you know to do, is sin. Relying on your own righteousness will prevent you from believing in the finished work of Jesus. Only by accepting the fact that our wasted effort of trying to live moral lives, striving to be good, and hating ourselves when we slip, will only draw us further away from grace. Per Galatians 5:4, "You who are trying to be justified by the law have been alienated from Christ; you have fallen away from grace."

Does that mean I shouldn't try being good, serving in church, and doing my spiritual disciplines? That is not what I am implying here. What I am trying to point to is your motivation. Why do you do those things? Is it to please God so He will not send you to hell? Is it to please others so they think highly of you as a Christian? Is it to prove that you are saved? Or is it because you are so overwhelmed by the gift Christ lavished on you, ransoming you from the penalty of all of your past, present, and future sins? When you realize the overwhelming grace God has lavished on you, you will be changed forever. Jesus said, "I have not come to call the righteous, but sinners to repentance" (Luke 5:32).

If you stopped doing all the things that you strive to do, would you still feel God's love for you? That is the real test of faith. Let's say you stopped reading and praying and going to church, would you feel God loved you? If not, then you are living a life of self-effort and trying to justify yourself by the law. You are alienated from Christ. The only way to be in Christ's family is to accept that there is nothing you can do to make Him love you more, and nothing you can do to make Him love you less. His love is constant, as we learned in Chapter Nine. No matter where life takes you, and what challenges come your way, God's love will never change toward you, and nothing will be able to separate you from His love, not even trying times. John 10:28 confirms this, "I give them eternal life, and they shall never perish; no one will snatch them out of my hand." I am not saying you should stop reading and praying, but once you learn about your motivation, you will see if you are living by faith or by work.

Do you believe that? If you do, then when you experience trials, consider how those trials demonstrate God's goodness and love for you. My trial with my last pregnancy gave me an opportunity to reflect on my own sin, the doubts I still had, and the misconceptions I still carried about God. But at the same time, it forced me to depend on God, to cry out to Him, and ask my church family to surround me with prayer. In the end, this trial became a ministry opportunity to speak about God's goodness even in the midst of trial. Most importantly, it taught me that all children, regardless of disability, are a gift from God, never a punishment. He uses everything for His glory. I no longer fear the idea of having a child with Down syndrome or any other disability because I know that God uses everything for my good, to make me more like Jesus.

Lie #11:	God will punish me for all my sins.
Truth #11:	**God punished His Son for all my sins.**

Before you turn the page to the last chapter, reflect on the following questions:

1. What trials have you experienced in your life?

2. What issues of the heart did God reveal to you through those trials?

3. How can you testify about God's goodness through the trials you experience?

Chapter 12

Regeneration

"And the God of all grace, who called you to his eternal glory in Christ, after you have suffered a little while, will himself restore you and make you strong, firm and steadfast."

— 1 Peter 5:10

Hi, my name is Nicole. I have a new life in Christ. God is recovering me from fear of failure, people-pleasing, perfectionism, pride, self-reliance, bitterness, anxiety, depression, eating disorder, co-dependency, anger, and trying to earn His favor and love. This was just the tip of the iceberg of the issues I had when I started Regeneration. When we met weekly with our group for the duration of about a year, we would introduce ourselves this way, but could only list three things at a time. Each week those three could change or stay the same, depending on what God was doing in our lives. When I started out in the program, I had no idea what my issues were, nor could I even admit them. I just knew I was not okay, and I could not fix myself. I was falling back to my old beliefs that came with my misunderstandings of God and His grace toward me.

Through this twelve-step program, I have reclaimed my identity and reaffirmed my belief. Each of the steps provided me an opportunity to re-evaluate what I believed, let go of the lies of the enemy, and embrace the truth of the gospel. This book was born as a result of the work God had done through the Regeneration program.

The first step was to admit that I was powerless to change myself. This was probably the hardest thing for me because I was pretty good at trying to fix and better myself—I had been doing it my whole life. I tried really hard to keep things under control, at least on the outside, so that people would accept me. I kept my weight controlled for the most part, kept going to school for more degrees, excelled in my job, tried to maintain good relationships with people, and worked hard to keep my faith alive through reading, prayer, church attendance, and serving. I tried to be the best version of myself, and to admit that I had shortcomings meant that I had to reveal the ugly truth to myself and others. But when I heard other ladies in this program share their struggles, I felt relieved because I was not the only one facing problems. I did not have to hide my insecurities and fears.

The second step was believing that God has the power to restore us. I learned through this step that my belief about God was impacting my behavior. As is often noted in the program, "Belief and action walk hand in hand. Our actions can show us how deeply we trust certain beliefs."[50] For example, if I believed that God is a distant, strict God, who is waiting for me to make a mistake so He can punish me, my behavior will be to walk on pins and needles, trying to not upset God, which will cause me to hate myself for not being perfect, and live in constant fear of failure. This describes most of my life. But if I believe God is a personal God, who loves me unconditionally, who wants only good for me, and who would go as far as to kill His own Son to save me from punishment and hell, my behavior will be different. I will have joy and desire in knowing this God and will trust Him with my life, letting Him do whatever He desires for His glory.

The third step was to trust God with our lives and our wills by accepting His grace through Jesus Christ. My biggest realization came when I discovered that I had trusted God with my eternity, because I didn't want to go to hell, but I struggled to trust Him in my daily life. This was due to my faulty belief that God was going to punish me, that He was angry with me when I failed to meet certain expectations, and that I was going to lose my salvation if I wasn't perfect when He came. Having this belief made it difficult for me to trust.

As a result, I was turning to other things for comfort, healing, and satisfaction. The program manual explains, "Jesus is more than an idea to agree with. He is a person to trust for eternity and abide with daily through every circumstance. He alone can save you and carry your burdens. Without Christ you cannot experience the full recovery that God wants for you."[51] Jesus states in John 15:5, "I am the vine; you are the branches. If you remain in me and I in you, you will bear much fruit; apart from me you can do nothing." So how do you remain in Jesus? I used to think it was by reading more Bible and not sinning, because it says in John 15:10, "If you keep my commands, you will remain in my love." I thought keeping commands was being sinless, so every time I sinned, I felt God no longer loved me. But then Jesus goes on to say in verse 12, "My command is this: Love each other as I have loved you." How does Jesus love us? When we're perfect? No, he loved and died for us while we were sinners[52] and he continues to love us as we become conformed to the image of His Son[53] through the process of sanctification.

The only way we can remain in God's love and love others the way he does is by having a personal relationship with Jesus. This happens when we acknowledge that there's nothing we can do to earn His favor and love (all religious activity) and nothing we can do to lose his favor and love (all our sins), which causes us to love the Lord with all our hearts, minds, and souls, which is the first and most important commandment.[54] So in order to remain in God's love, we should love God and love people. The way we love God is by accepting His gift and the way we love people is by loving them as they are and bringing the message of hope to them through our redemption story. Galatians 5:14 says that the entire law is fulfilled by keeping this commandment of loving your neighbor.

The fourth step was probably the most impactful one for me. I had to make a moral inventory of all of my past, including all my bitterness toward individuals and institutions, my fears, all harms done to me and by me, my sexual history, and my recovery issues. This thorough analysis of my thoughts, actions, and motives helped me discover patterns about my behavior and my idols. I learned that all of my behavior was rooted in my belief about who I was and my distrust of who God was. I realized I was still living under the old covenant of the law in some ways, which was really difficult to get rid of, instead of living in Christ. It says in 2 Corinthians 3:14, "But their minds were made dull, for to this day the same veil remains when the old covenant is read. It has not been removed, because only in Christ is it taken away." I could not experience an intimate relationship with the Lord because of my rule-following mentality that if I didn't wear the right clothes, or didn't pray a certain way, or didn't know enough of the Bible, I wasn't a good enough Christian. A good visual for that is a wedding ceremony when the groom lifts the bride's veil to kiss her. If the bride refuses to lift the veil (religious mentality), they could never be intimate. I felt that every night because I would lay down and feel guilty for not getting on my knees to pray. It had to be on my knees or God wouldn't hear as well. Once I started renewing my mind with the truth about who I was and about who God was, my relationship with Christ took on a whole different flavor.

The fifth step was to confess all of my inventory to another person—someone I would choose as my mentor. I had a hard time deciding who to ask to be my mentor because I did not trust anyone with my painful past nor my shameful present; I think the reason for this was I did not know anyone in my church who had struggled with any issues, so I didn't think anyone would ever understand me. I was afraid of being judged and rejected. Nonetheless, I took a risk with one of my friends, who had been a little more open with me than most, and I felt like I could trust her. I met with her weekly for the duration of the program, something I am really grateful for. As I confessed everything to her, it felt symbolic to laying all of my guilt and shame at the feet of Jesus and allowing Him use it for His glory.

The sixths step was to repent from our patterns of sin and turn to God. The most important lesson learned here was that you *can't* just stop your patterns of sinning, though you might be able to control it. What you *can* do is turn away from your sin and turn toward God. For example, if I am prone to yelling at my kids when I am angry or have just had enough, then I need to make a plan for how I am going to turn to God when I feel the need to yell. To do this, I had to analyze my triggers, the times I was most vulnerable, the places I frequently struggled, why I struggled, and how I was tempted to struggle. With that analysis, I was able to create a plan of how I was going to make changes so that I could turn away from sin and instead turn to Christ. This was liberating because only through Christ's power can we ever overcome our sin patterns.

The seventh step was to commit to following Christ as His Spirit changes our hearts and minds. The most important revelation here was that trying to change myself by my own effort was senseless. Only by following Jesus and being empowered by Him are we able to truly experience freedom from our old ruts. Apostle Paul speaks to Galatians about this topic because they were turning back to the law after they had received the Spirit. Galatians 3:3 says, "Are you so foolish? After beginning by means of the Spirit, are you now trying to finish by means of the flesh?"

I was a foolish Galatian who, after receiving the Spirit, continued relying on my own works for my sanctification and maturity. We cannot do both. We either live by faith, or we live by our own effort in trying to receive freedom from our sinful patterns. It would be equivalent to keeping one foot on a moving treadmill and one foot on the floor—impossible. It is also impossible to live by faith and by your own effort relying on your own works. Here is an excerpt from my workbook,

"Your sinful nature and the lures of the world are, however, not too strong for God. Just as God offers himself to you as the way to freedom, he also offers himself as the means to freedom. Since God's love, mercy, strength, and sacrifice rescued you from sin in the first place, then it follows that only God can satisfy your needs. He will carry you forward. Delighting in God and relying upon him is how to experience freedom."[55]

The way that the Holy Spirt works in us is by spending time in God's word, memorizing His promises by storing them in your heart, and spending time in prayer while listening to Him speak. Have you ever just paused while praying and listened to what God had to say? Or have you ever written questions in your journal and then started reading the Bible to hear God answer? Following the Holy Spirit's guidance not only helps us grow spiritually, but it is also refreshing and exciting because God is not a boring God, as I used to think when I was a child. It is also important to spend time with God's people and be part of a community group so that you are able to grow together with other Christians.

The eighth step was about forgiveness. This seemed like an easy step. After all, I thought I had forgiven all the people who had hurt me in the past. However, what I learned when I was trying to complete this step was that I still had bitterness and resentment toward some of the people I'd forgiven. Though I had told myself that I had forgiven, someplace deep inside, I still held on to pain. Through my workbook, I learned about true forgiveness, which is "an unconditional transaction between you and God—a decision to release to God both the damage of sin and your demands for justice. Forgiveness does not depend upon your offender's presence, response, understanding, or repentance. When you transfer sin to God, you do not excuse the sin, but honestly acknowledge its debt and accept God's judgment of it and vengeance upon it as your own. Forgiveness is a work of the Holy Spirit in you to trust God and to love others with Christ's love."[56]

I had to go through my entire inventory and, with each situation and individual that/who had caused me harm, release the debt to God. This was another powerful activity I have done as part of this program—transferring all the debts of sin against me onto God by writing them all down on a cross depicted in my book. I listed all my pain suffered and rejection received and placed it all at the feet of Jesus. Forgiveness allowed me to start seeing people as Christ sees them, all in need of love and grace.

The ninth step involved making amends to people who I had harmed. In my workbook, I learned that making amends is God's way of helping us reconcile relationships, which is what God desires for us. "Biblical amends makes no excuses for your sin and carries no expectation of receiving any good in return from those whom you have hurt. It can only be done as you follow Christ, humbly trusting God to carry you through any outcome."[57] This was probably the most difficult step and, for various reasons, the only step I have not completed fully. I started by making amends with my immediate family.

One of the most amazing things that has happened through this process was that by humbly admitting my shortcomings and sins, especially toward my own children, I was able to experience overwhelming grace and open the door to authentic conversation. I did this individually with my oldest daughters and have also done this with my husband. I hope someday I will have an opportunity to do this with other people I have harmed. If you are reading this and you are one of those people, I am truly sorry. There is no excuse for my behavior or what I have done to you. I want to be better, do better, and love better, just as Christ loves me. Maybe one day I can say this to you over coffee.

The tenth step was about learning to follow God on a daily basis. Recovery in Christ is not a onetime event, but a lifelong journey as the Holy Spirit continues to change us so we look more like Jesus. It is about relying on God daily, rather than on your own strength and power. 1 Peter 2:16 says, "Live as free people, but do not use your freedom as a cover-up for evil; live as God's slaves." This step is all about doing steps one through nine on an ongoing basis. Here is an excerpt from my workbook: "Remember, as long as you live in this world, sin will affect you. You will experience hardship and others will hurt you. You will be tempted to find more pleasure, peace, and purpose in creation than from your Creator. Satan will try to draw you away from God and limit the effectiveness of God's purpose for you."[58] The way the devil usually draws me away is by pulling me back into religious mentality that I must do something to earn God's favor or I could do something to lose His favor. I have to constantly repent of this mentality and believe God's truth that I'm saved by grace through faith in Jesus Christ.

This step has taught me not to let down my guard but to stand against the enemy's schemes that aim to distract, disarm, and destroy me. As Ephesians 6:10-12 reminds us, we must put on the full armor of God. "Finally, be strong in the Lord and in his mighty power. Put on the full armor of God, so that you can take your stand against the devil's schemes. For our struggle is not against flesh and blood, but against the rulers, against the authorities, against the powers of this dark world and against the spiritual forces of evil in the heavenly realms." This passage goes on to describe the weapons that we must use to take our stand, which include the *belt of truth, breastplate of righteousness, gospel of peace, shield of faith, helmet of salvation,* and the *sword of the Spirit,* which is the word of God. Notice that all of these words have to do with the gift of grace given to us through Jesus Christ by faith. Even in the face of setback, I have learned to quickly get up and continue following Jesus, without wallowing in my sin, feeling sorry for myself, and thinking that God is angry with me. Knowing God loves me unconditionally allows me to quickly turn away from my sin and follow Christ.

The eleventh step took me through understanding what it means to have an intimate relationship with Jesus. Growing up, I never understood this concept. I never felt intimacy with God until I started seeing Him as a loving Father who loves me unconditionally. God promises us an abundant life filled with peace, joy, and satisfaction, which are all found in the person Jesus, not in anything else this world has to offer, but only in Him. Philippians 3:7-11 describes how Apostle Paul saw Jesus, "But whatever were gains to me I now consider loss for the sake of Christ. What is more, I consider everything a loss because of the surpassing worth of knowing Christ Jesus my Lord, for whose sake I have lost all things. I consider them garbage, that I may gain Christ and be found in him, not having a righteousness of my own that comes from the law, but that which is through faith in Christ—the righteousness that comes from God, on the basis of faith. I want to know Christ and the power of his resurrection and participation in his sufferings, becoming like him in his death, and so, somehow, attaining to the resurrection from the dead." For Paul, Jesus was the ultimate prize, more precious than anything else, and not just for Paul, we also see David in the book of Psalms praise Him throughout the book. Psalm 73:25-26 says, "Whom have I in heaven but you? And earth has nothing I desire but you. My flesh and my heart may fail, but God is the strength of my heart, and my portion forever."

Are there things that you do to earn rewards in heaven? I often hear of people doing things for other people because they want to be compensated in heaven. Yes, the Bible does teach to store up treasures in heaven as we read in Mathew 6:19-21, "Do not store up for yourselves treasures on earth, where moths and venom destroy, where thieves break in and steal. But store up for yourselves treasures in heaven, where moths and vermin do not destroy, and where thieves do not break in and steal. For where your treasure is, there your heart will be also." Heaven is a great motivator to do nice things for others, but what kinds of rewards are you looking to get in heaven? Sure, there will be rewards, but if Jesus is not enough of a reward, you might be missing the point. Jesus is the ultimate prize that we have because heaven will not be heaven without Jesus. When we are in Christ, we will be in heaven, wherever and whatever it will be. Jesus wants all your affections toward Him.

The very last step called, Regenerate, was about sharing your testimony about God's grace to help reconcile others to God. Here is an excerpt from my workbook that speaks to this point:

"Jesus is alive! He is actively rescuing people today. The difference between when Jesus walked on earth and now is that today he rescues sinners through his Spirit living in the sons and daughters of God—you. God does not heal you and free you from your sinful nature so that you can just move on with your own plans, living your life unbothered by trouble. God bought you with Christ's blood, so that you can participate in God's rescue plan for others."[59]

God can use anyone and everyone who has been changed by Jesus's sacrifice to help Him bring more people to faith. I have written this entire book to share my journey of faith for one purpose: to testify about a God that is relentless in pursuing sinners, those who continually rebel against Him, yet He still loves them. He wants to take away your shame and give you grace instead. It took me almost my entire life to learn how much God really loved me all along. I faced obstacles throughout my life and made regretful mistakes, sinning against God, yet He never gave up on me. And He will not give up on you. He loves you and has a plan for you.

Do not let your pride hold you back from surrendering to Him, letting go of your fruitless efforts of trying to save yourself, whether through religious activity or just good works. Neither one is enough. God wants your heart, filled with faith that His sacrifice was enough to pay your penalty and give you freedom to live in Him and for Him by faith. All you have to do is receive it! If you have received it, continue living by faith the same way you received it. It is an ongoing journey of faith. Let me pray for you.

Dear heavenly Father, I am grateful that You have given me this opportunity to share my story of redemption. I thank You for every person who has taken a chance on this book, but more importantly, taken on chance to hear about Your great and mighty work that You continue to do in the lives of people. I pray that these truths will bring healing and hope into the life of every reader. I pray they would be encouraged to share their own story about Your amazing grace. Please empower them with Your strength, Your power, Your peace, and Your love so that they will not rest until they proclaim Your Great Name to this broken world that so desperately needs You. I pray this in Your Son's Holy Name. Amen!

Lie #12:	God will give up on me if I keep messing up.
Truth #12:	**God will never give up on me.**

Reflect on the following questions:

1. What lies did you believe that prevented you from experiencing freedom in Christ?

2. What truth impacted you the most? How?

3. How will you use these truths in your circle of influence to lead people to freedom in Christ?

Conclusion

To Freedom in Christ

> "Now the Lord is the Spirit, and where the
> Spirit of the Lord is, there is freedom."
>
> **— 2 Corinthians 3:17**

Freedom! What do you think about when you hear this word? It holds different connotations for different people. In my experience growing up in a legalistic environment with so many strict rules for behavior, *freedom* had a negative connotation. It was considered recklessness if someone were to say, "I am free in Christ." It is a dangerous word because it gives people the idea that they can do whatever they want, including sin. This is why it was so important to prescribe so many rules about behavior. If people had freedom, they would cause havoc on their lives.

To me, this word means something different. It means that I can finally rest in the beautiful gospel of Christ that gives me full assurance of my salvation. It does not mean that I am free to sin, but rather free from sin because I am no longer under the old covenant of the law. Even though I am not under the law, the last thing I want to do is cause destruction to myself and live in misery, as I did most of my life. Sin leads to destruction and if I understand that, there is no possible way I would want to commit sin on purpose, just because it is paid for. Instead, since my sin and shame are nailed to the cross, I can live on purpose for God, testifying to His amazing grace, which can save, heal, and empower. I don't have to stress over messing up and then beat myself up for my failure. I can rest in knowing that I am in His hands as I repent and turn away from my sins. Most importantly I am able to grow and mature as a Christian while ministering to others about this hope in Christ.

Freedom in Christ allows me to live in a relationship, not focused on following religious duties. This is still a challenge sometimes as most of my life I lived legalistically. I read the Bible and prayed out of guilt or as a check off item on my list, rather than out of thirst to connect with Jesus. Now, whenever I think that I *have* to read or pray, or something bad will happen, I repent of these thoughts and bring them to God, asking Him to continue healing me of this mentality. Whenever I serve or do ministry out of *duty* rather than out of joy, I stop doing it. I do not want my relationship with God to be mechanical and dead. I never want to sing one song without my heart fully present and alive. I never want to pray one prayer just because I need to pray before bed or over food. I want my actions to come from the heart, not out of religious duty.

All the lies I believed did not allow me to experience true freedom in Christ, causing me to doubt my salvation and live in bondage to sin. True freedom only happens when we believe the truth about who God is and who we are in Him. It is absolutely impossible to experience freedom in Christ through legalism—strict following of self-created rules. I have learned that the hard way. I had to let go of my legalistic tendencies and embrace the life of faith though a relationship with Jesus. As a result, I now live free from the addictive tendencies I used to cope with my guilt and shame.

In November of 2018, I rededicated my life to Jesus through a water baptism in the church where I went through the Regeneration program. It was an experience I will never forget. I snuck out of the house to attend a morning service, this time without my husband because he was working. I needed to be at my own church immediately after this service, so I was already dressed, with my hair and makeup done. The sermon was about Jesus getting baptized to fulfill all righteousness, and as I listened, I started thinking I needed to get re-baptized. I had wanted to for a while. I felt like when I was seventeen, I got baptized out of religious duty, but now, twenty years later, it would be because I entered into a relationship with Jesus by faith. Religious baptism felt like an arranged marriage—without intimacy—but now it was true love. I loved Jesus with all my heart and understood how much he loved me and what He had done to save me. I had finally taken off the veil of living under the old covenant of the law and entered into an intimate relationship with Him. But there was a battle going on inside me with voices from my flesh and the Spirit.

Flesh: *You already did your hair, you wouldn't want to get it messy again, and it looks so good.*

Spirit: *It's just hair, who cares, at least you are wearing all black today, perfect for baptism, nothing will be see-through. Today's the perfect day for it.*

Flesh: *You are going to get wet, how will you drive home? Vadim will kill you for getting his leather seats wet.*

Spirit: *Vadim would be fine when he learns it's baptism water.*

Flesh: *But you will be late to the Russian service. You need to leave early. Baptism will be toward the end of church. Plus, you have to go home and change.*

Spirit: *What's more important? Attending two services or doing My will?*

I decided to obey the Spirit and stayed. I told God I was only going to come out when I felt the Spirit move me through a song. Two songs passed and I didn't feel anything; then, the third song played, and it spoke about coming out of the grave. Its words pushed me forward as if I were getting out of the grave into a new life. I went up to the front, told the lady I wanted to re-dedicate my life of faith, and was in the baptismal pool immediately getting baptized with a renewed understanding of God's grace. I was the only one baptized that service! It was all set up just for me! It was amazing! The lights were in my face, as if it were just me and God in heaven, with people celebrating in the background. No more lies. No more shame. I am a child of God, saved by grace, through faith in Jesus Christ.

As a result of God's work in my life, I found overwhelming peace, complete healing, and eternal hope. Since I cannot be quiet about the transforming power of the gospel, I am now seeing the change in my husband and in my kids, as they share how God is working in their hearts and freeing them from the destructive cycle of sin and shame. I am witnessing a difference in my friends as their conversations shift from surface talk to discussions about the issues of the heart and God's work in their life. Our church is evolving too. We now realize how some traditions could be an obstacle to those who need the gospel the most, so we adopted a vision that focuses on hospitality to welcome everyone. This way people could hear the gospel and come to know the Lord Jesus Christ. Are we perfect? No, but we are striving to become the church God created us to be, which is to bind the broken-hearted, bring freedom to the captives, healing to the sick, and most importantly hope to those who feel hopeless. When new believers get baptized in our church, we encourage them to share their testimony of how they came to Christ, and we do not expect them to be perfect the next day, as we know it is God who changes hearts. Our job as a church is to help believers transform their minds through the truth of the gospel, and that truth will set them free from their old patterns of sin, rooted in the lies they believed about themselves and about God.

I hope that through this book, you have discovered the lies you believed and learned the truth about what it means to be free in Christ and live by faith, not works. I pray that these truths continue to deliver you from bondage to sin and shame, because the enemy does not sleep. He is constantly feeding you lies. Resist the enemy by meditating on God's truths and remembering that Jesus took care of your shame, as Hebrews 12:1-2 says, "And let us run with perseverance the race marked out for us, fixing our eyes on Jesus, the pioneer and perfecter of faith. For the joy set before him he endured the cross, scorning its shame, and sat down at the right hand of the throne of God." I pray that you use your freedom to bring the gospel of peace, healing and hope to the people in your life and to the world around you. This world needs these truths now more than ever before.

Truth #1:	Jesus is the only solution for my brokenness.
Truth #2:	I will still struggle with sin after coming to Christ.
Truth #3:	There is nothing I need to do to earn acceptance from God.
Truth #4:	I confess my sin so I can have an intimate relationship with God and others.
Truth #5:	Jesus is the only one who can fill my need for love.
Truth #6:	Jesus paid for my past, present, and future sins.
Truth #7:	I can only please God by faith.
Truth #8:	God's love is constant and does not depend on my behavior.
Truth #9:	Believing the truth in the Bible will transform my life.
Truth #10:	God wants me to testify about Him through my redemption story.
Truth #11:	God punished His Son for all my sins.
Truth #12:	God will never give up on me.

Acknowledgments

I would like to thank those in my life whose prayers, encouragement, and unyielding faith have made this book a possibility.

Vadim, your love and grace have transformed me in so many ways and continue to do so. You never fail to be my biggest supporter. Thank you for giving me the space and time to write, as you tirelessly took care of our house and kids. You never once complained! I am grateful for your confidence in me and your love that propels me to share the good news of the gospel of grace.

My girls (Alena, Yana, Lilly, Sofia), I am so grateful for your patience and understanding as you watched your mom lock herself in her room your whole summer break. Thank you for your support as you cheered me on in persevering through the obstacles in publishing this book. I love you all so much.

Philip, thank you for your sweet, gentle kisses that kept me pushing through. Your little voice every morning saying, "Mommy, it's your baby boy, who brings you so much joy!" energized me and warmed my heart.

Thank you to all my prayer warriors in my Bible study group. You have always been my backbone. This book has become a reality because of your love and acceptance of me. I love you with all of my heart and pray that you continue to run after Jesus and help many more people find healing and hope in Him.

Thank you to my Fresno church family for your love and grace. You encourage me to keep going and pressing on. I love you all!

Thank you to The Bridge Church, and the staff that ministered to my kids Sunday after Sunday. You played a big role in my life in helping me understand God's grace and ministering to me in my most challenging season of life. May the Lord continue to bless you in all that you do!

Thank you to my family, siblings, and parents for loving me no matter what. I know it was not an easy journey for you, but I am grateful for your sacrifice. I love you more than you will ever know. I want all my family to be free from destructiveness of sin that had plagued our family for generations. God has the power to do that if we let him.

Thank you to Natasha, for being my friend for life and walking this journey with me. Your genuine love and grace compel me. Thank you for being my evangelistic partner when we were young. Thank you for being the one to invite me to Fresno. Also, thank you for taking a chance on me and inviting me to speak, though you knew nothing about my past. You have opened the door to my healing and eventually to God's work to proclaim His message of reconciliation and hope.

ACKNOWLEDGMENTS

Thank you to The Well Church and all the ladies in my Regeneration circle, who spent a year with me, helping me process my past and present. Thank you for your encouragement, prayers, and love. I love you very much!

Thank you, Inna, for being my mentor through Regeneration experience. You had given me so much of your time and heart loving me through it all. I am grateful that you were transparent with me to open the door to my vulnerability. It was a healing process and I will never forget this.

Thank you to my mentor Jennifer Hayes Yates. You were God sent to me and have embraced me with open arms. You have helped me in this process of book publishing that I knew nothing about. Your prayers, encouragement, and commitment to sharing the gospel kept me going even in the face of opposition. I hope one day I get to meet you in person so we can chat over coffee.

Thank you to Self-Publishing School and Mastermind Community who have guided me through the process of publishing this book. Without you, I'd be lost. Your feedback, encouragement, and wisdom are greatly appreciated.

Most importantly, thank you Jesus for lifting me out of my pit of despair and giving me a firm foundation to stand on. I love You with all my mind, heart, soul, and strength! Keep molding me and using me for your glory. I am forever Yours.

About Nicole Gorban

Nicole Gorban is a wife, mom, educator, and speaker who loves God and people. She enjoys reading, writing, traveling, and drinking coffee. She takes an active part in leading women's ministry at her church in Fresno, California, and was recently selected to be an assistant of women's ministry in the Pacific Coast Slavic Baptist Association. She has a passion for ministering to girls and women and encouraging them to live a life of purpose for the Lord. Aside from her church ministry, she currently serves as a Vice Principal of an elementary school, where she enjoys being the hands and feet of Jesus, loving and supporting students, teachers, and families.

Nicole's mission is to bring people healing and hope through the power of God's grace found in a relationship with Jesus Christ. She is passionate about bringing glory to God by sharing her redemption journey and encouraging others to share theirs. She believes that by fully grasping the gospel and the love of God, people can find true freedom from guilt and shame, which is essential for the growth and maturity of every Christian.

You can connect with Nicole through her blog at http://authentic-faith.blog or her email at nicolegorban30@gmail.com

Thank You for Reading My Book!

I really appreciate all of your feedback, and I love hearing what you have to say.

If you were blessed by reading *Grace Over Shame*, please consider leaving a review on Amazon.

Thanks so much!

Nicole

NOW IT'S YOUR TURN

Discover the EXACT 3-step blueprint you need to become a bestselling author in as little as 3 months.

Self-Publishing School helped me, and now I want them to help you with this FREE resource to begin outlining your book!

Even if you're busy, bad at writing, or don't know where to start, you CAN write a bestseller and build your best life.

With tools and experience across a variety of niches and professions, Self-Publishing School is the <u>only</u> resource you need to take your book to the finish line!

DON'T WAIT

Say "YES" to becoming a bestseller:

https://self-publishingschool.com/friend/

Follow the steps on the page to get a FREE resource to get started on your book and unlock a discount to get started with Self-Publishing School

Endnotes

[1] Brené Brown, *I Thought it was Just Me (But it Isn't): Making the Journey from "What Will People Think?" to "I Am Enough"* (New York: NY, Penguin, 2007), 5.

[2] Timothy Keller, *The Reason for God and The Prodigal God* (New York, NY: Penguin, 2008), 183.

[3] Ibid., 183-184.

[4] Wikipedia contributors, "Persecution of Christians in the Soviet Union," *Wikipedia, The Free Encyclopedia*, https://en.wikipedia.org/w/index.php?title=Persecution_of_Christians_in_the_Soviet_Union&oldid=956728883 (accessed June 10, 2020).

[5] The movie can be found at https://www.youtube.com/watch?v=wk2MBnPgbcI.

[6] 1 Timothy 5:23

[7] Ezekiel 16:11-12

[8] Psalm 47:1-2

[9] Psalm 149:3

[10] 2 Samuel 11-12.

[11] 1 Chronicles 21:1, "Satan rose up against Israel and incited David to take a census of Israel."

[12] 1 Samuel 20:6, "If your father misses me at all, tell him, 'David earnestly asked my permission to hurry to Bethlehem, his hometown, because an annual sacrifice is being made there for his whole clan.'"

[13] Psalm 55:12-14, "If an enemy were insulting me, I could endure it; if a foe were rising himself against me, I could hide from him. But it is you, a man like myself, my companion, my close friend, with whom I once enjoyed sweet fellowship at the house of God, as we walked about among the worshippers."

[14] Matthew 26:35.

[15] Matthew 26:69-70, "Now Peter was sitting out in the courtyard, and a servant girl came to him. 'You also were with Jesus of Galilee,' she said. But he denied it before them all. 'I don't know what you're talking about,' he said."

[16] Romans 7:15, "I do not understand what I do. For what I want to do I do not do, but what I hate I do."

[17] Brown, *I Thought*, 14.

[18] Mark W. Baker, *Overcoming Shame* (2018), 15.

[19] Exodus 3:17, "And I have promised to bring you up out of your misery in Egypt into the land of the Canaanites, Hittites, Amorites, Perizzites, Hivites and Jebusites—a land flowing with milk and honey."

[20] Kim M. Baldwin, John R. Baldwin, and Thomas Ewald, "The Relationship among Shame, Guild, and Self-Efficacy," *American Journal of Psychotherapy*, 60, 1 (2006),1-20, file:///Users/vadimgorban/Downloads/RelamongShameGuiltandSelf-Efficancy%20(1).pdf.

[21] Baldwin, Baldwin, and Ewald, *The Relationship*, 17.

[22] Isaiah 64:6.

[23] Matthew 7:15-23.

[24] John Lynch, Bruce McNicol, and Bill Thrall, *The Cure* (San Clemente: CA, CrossSection, 2011), 12-18.

[25] Lynch, McNicol, and Thrall, *The Cure*, 15.

[26] 1 John 5:16-17.

[27] Matthew 16:6, "Be on your guard against the yeast of the Pharisees and Sadducees." Matthew 16:12, "Then they

understood that he was not telling them to guard against the yeast used in bread, but against the teaching of the Pharisees and Sadducees."

[28] James 1:27, 2:3-4, 2:8.

[29] 1 Peter 3:21.

[30] 1 Timothy 3:2-5.

[31] Mark 3:21.

[32] Dorothy Kelley Patterson, Rhonda Harrington Kelley, and Homan Bible Staff, *The Study Bible for Women: Holman Christian Standards Bible* (Tennessee: B&H Publishing Group, 2015), 1401.

[33] F. Remy Diederich, *Healing the Hurts of Your Past: A Guide to Overcoming the Pain of Shame* (2006), 23.

[34] Diederich, *Healing the Hurts*, 34-109.

[35] Ibid., 86.

[36] Ibid., 91-95.

[37] Ibid., 102-107.

[38] John Piper, *What is Sin? The Essence and Root of All Sinning*, 2015.

[39] Ibid., 2015.

[40] Eating Disorder Coalition, *Fact Sheet*, https://www.eatingdisorderscoalition.org.

[41] Exodus 15:22.

[42] Exodus 16:16.

[43] Exodus 32:1-14.

[44] John 8:33.

[45] Philip Yancey, *What's So Amazing about Grace?* (Grand Rapids: MI, Zondervan, 1997), 70.

[46] *Holy Bible: New Living Translation* (Wheaton, Illinois: Tyndale House Publishers, 2004).

[47] Colossians 1:13.

[48] John 4:39.

[49] Luke 7:41-42.

[50] *Re:generation Recovery – Realize Your Need for God's Grace: Steps 1-3* (Dallas: TX, Watermark Community Church, 2016), 41.

[51] Ibid., 102.

[52] Romans 5:8.

[53] Romans 8:29.

[54] Matthew 22:37.

[55] *Re:generation – Respond to God's Grace: Steps 7-9* (Dallas: TX, Watermark Community Church, 2016), 13.

[56] Ibid., 65.

[57] Ibid., 81.

[58] *Re:generation – Because of God's Grace: Steps 10-12* (Dallas: TX, Watermark Community Church, 2016), 14.

[59] Ibid., 75.